Heart Flame
Healing

A Journey of Healing, Regeneration & Co Creation with the Divine

KARIN INANA

BALBOA.
PRESS

A DIVISION OF HAY HOUSE

Balboa Press books may be ordered through booksellers or by contacting:

Balboa Press
A Division of Hay House
1663 Liberty Drive
Bloomington, IN 47403
www.balboapress.com
1 (877) 407-4847

Because of the dynamic nature of the Internet, any web addresses or
links contained in this book may have changed since publication and may
no longer be valid. The views expressed in this work are solely those
of the author and do not necessarily reflect the views of the publisher,
and the publisher hereby disclaims any responsibility for them.

The author of this book does not dispense medical advice or prescribe the use
of any technique as a form of treatment for physical, emotional, or medical
problems without the advice of a physician, either directly or indirectly. The
intent of the author is only to offer information of a general nature to help
you in your quest for emotional and spiritual well-being. In the event you use
any of the information in this book for yourself, which is your constitutional
right, the author and the publisher assume no responsibility for your actions.

Any people depicted in stock imagery provided by Getty Images are
models, and such images are being used for illustrative purposes only.
Certain stock imagery © Getty Images.

Print information available on the last page.

ISBN: 978-1-9822-1476-0 (sc)
ISBN: 978-1-9822-1478-4 (hc)
ISBN: 978-1-9822-1477-7 (e)

Library of Congress Control Number: 2018912791

Balboa Press rev. date: 05/15/2019

For my parents and my family
of the sacred human heart

Longing, as defined by *Merriam-Webster*, is a strong desire, a yearning, especially for something unattainable. This is not the kind of longing I am talking about here.

The Sacred Longing of the Human Heart

The kind of longing I am writing about is the tender feeling residing in your upper chest, the place where we tend to put our hands when talking about something that really deeply matters to us. Tuning into this longing, we are instantly connected to the very thing that animates our physical existence, our subtle energetic spirit body. It is this longing in the upper chest, also called the *soul seat* that has the power to transform your life—to make it what you dream of—because it is intimately connected to your spirit and to the purpose of your life. Here in your soul seat resides the very reason you have chosen to take a physical body this time around. It is your *inner heart's dream*—that which you came here to do, be, and experience. Your *sacred longing* is the guiding light on the road to the fulfillment of your life. And it is absolutely attainable.

Heart Flame Healing

Heart flame healing is the process of moving into the *wholeness of your life*, guided by your sacred longing, the spiritual flame burns with the ultimate desire to fulfill your life, rising from the depth within your heart of hearts. It is your inner heart's dream. The thing you long most for (at any point in your life) also longs for you—it longs to be fulfilled.

What is the MDST (Multidimensional Support Team)?

The MDST is a team of beings made up of deities, spirit guides, spirit surgeons, angelic beings, ascended masters, and other humans that are embodied or not. They are living light aspects of God, or the unlimited source from which all things spring forth; and they are in service to humanity. They mostly reside in the unseen subtle energy realm but some of them are also alive on earth, in service to the greater good of all.

Every person who works in support of "the greater good of all" has a team available. The more extensive your task the bigger your team! It is safe to say that all leaders, teachers, and doctors have guides, even if they don't know it (or, perhaps, don't even believe in them). If you have a job in the service of others and for the greater good for all, you have divine guidance available to you. As a matter fact, divine guidance is available to all who ask for it.

Contents

Acknowledgments

A special thanks to all those who have contributed directly or indirectly to the completion of *Heart Flame Healing*. To Tilli, with much gratitude from the depth of my heart, I am not sure I could have done it without your input and help. Gunnar, thank you for reading my manuscript in all states of progress and for being the wonderful friend that you are to me. Heidi thanks for your relentless encouragement and for sharing the journey with me through all the ups and downs. To Greta Hassel Grace, Dennis Cohen, Heidi Funk, Michael Glock, Rochelle Cook, Charlotte Reznick, Bobby Brown, Kate and Elliot Anders, Bruce Miller, Joe Banz, my Mr. Whiskers, Jessica Schaefer, Robert I., Kevin Ryan, and Dr. David Saperia for reading my manuscript. Thanks to each of you for your unique support, love, and friendship. It means the world to me. Also thanks to all my wonderful clients and students for placing your trust in me. I have learned so much from each of you, and I love you all.

Preface

As I began the journey of writing this guidebook, I thought about my longing, past and present. While sharing with a friend, I realized how easily and naturally I had manifested some of my (true) inner heart's desire. I remembered that, at eighteen years old, while working and going to school, I lamented the rigid work schedules that governed everyone's life, including mine. Work above all else was what determined a good German life. As my adult life was fast approaching, I felt trapped by this automatic agreement and adherence to the forty-hour work week as a way of life. I wanted the freedom to enjoy my life. What if I desired to play or make love in the middle of the day? What if I wanted to work more hours one day and fewer the next? What if an artistic inspiration came over me in the middle of the day? I longed to be free to heed the call of divine inspiration and could not find anything wrong with my desire. Another huge part of my yearning was to live near the ocean, to watch the waves, smell the fragrant ocean air, play in the water, walk along the beach, and enjoy the distant sounds of the waves crashing against the shore at night. Within all of this, I also had a strong desire for my life to count and to make sense.

I longed to know God within myself, to help others and to have the freedom to enjoy my life. I now lived this life, free and on my own terms, with the Pacific Ocean in view even as I wrote these words.

In fact, I was obsessed by this feeling of longing, too strong to be ignored even though there was an elusive quality to it—a dreamer's world, easily dismissed (by the rational mind) as a pie in the sky. Yet I could not shake this feeling; I had to look there—to feel the sensation in the upper part of my chest below my sternum and then this fire in my belly. The feeling was incredibly strong; I was fascinated by it. I spent hours in my room, focusing on that sensation in my body—a feeling in my heart and soul that drew me deep inside a dark yet warm and fertile place. Without knowing what I was doing in those hours, I connected to and honored the sacred longing of my inner heart's dream by listening deeply.

I had forgotten about that particular period of my life until just now. From that moment on I was guided to fulfill my heart's desire, and to follow my sacred longing became the most important thing in my life. It was a natural process but not directed by the rational mind. On the contrary, at times I made decisions on the spot that seemed irrational—like getting on a plane by myself and journeying to a foreign country (the United States) without properly speaking the language or knowing how to provide for myself. Yet driven by this fire in my belly, so much so that I never considered failure, I managed to manifest what I so desired. I now lived this life, free on my own terms. I lived close to the Pacific Ocean, and for many years I had the big blue in view first thing every morning, right from my bedroom window. While writing this book, I had manifested another deep longing of mine, which I will share with you later.

And yes, work still governs my life more than anything else, but I love what I do and cannot imagine being without this essential expression of my inner essence. It is my joy and pleasure to fulfill my purpose in being an active healing presence in this world. I am happy to be of service for the greater good of all, as doing so gives me my life of choice.

Since my arrival in the United States, I have become a successful healer with a global healing practice. I provide high-level healing services to my clients, repairing the human aura by removing distortions, blockages, and traumas; helping to restore optimum flow of life force energy to their auras and physical bodies; and, thereby, helping to heal body, mind, and spirit naturally.

I do this work together with the assistance and support of a team of spiritual light beings. I call them my multidimensional support team or MDST. I have cultivated my relationship with these generous light beings consciously, over the last two decades, and I could not do this sacred work without my MDST team. I have now been in practice for over twenty years and have assisted thousands of clients locally and globally, to heal their bodies and their lives.

I am writing so that my voice will be heard, to fulfill my longing, and to share my knowledge. I am writing for you—you, who came upon these words by way of your own desire for healing.

Whatever it is that needs healing, it usually starts with a feeling that something is not right, a sensation of pain or maybe a feeling of deep dissatisfaction. Any of these signals, if they go on long enough, will move us to seek a way out of the painful predicament.

My current predicament, challenge, or discontent at the time of writing had everything to do with this book (the one you are holding in your hand right now), which had been a longing of mine for some time. Now however, it had become intolerable not to write. I went from avoidance and procrastination to serious suffering, enough to finally move me into action. Thank God, now I could breathe easier.

Signaled by the feeling of something missing, a "divine discontent" increasingly nagging and becoming more painful with every passing day. Finally I allowed the feeling and felt consciously that something was missing, my guidebook for my healing practice. I needed it; my clients needed it; humanity needed it; and most likely you, my dear friend, need it too. It needed to be available. It was already inside of me, wanting to get out and creating a great deal of internal pressure, an emotional manifestation akin to anxiety. Perhaps you are familiar with this feeling?

If you are reading *Heart Flame Healing*, you know that I have succeeded and fulfilled one of my longings; I have written this book—the one you are reading. Even though doing so wasn't always easy, I followed through all the way, and I am happy that this book is now in your hands.

Please allow me to help you fulfill your inner heart's dream, healing intention, or longing. I would like to guide you in your heart flame healing journey—a journey of healing, rejuvenation, and regeneration and the ultimate claiming of your birthright as a fully creative being (of God), which is the *power to heal yourself*! Now I know that is a mouthful, but I mean it. Yes, we do have this power. But we have to claim and exercise this God-given right to bring it fully into action. *Heart Flame Healing* is a roadmap, and your inner heart's dream is where the journey starts.

Who am I to write this book?

I am an ordinary woman with an extraordinary life task. Over time, have become more and more of who I really am. I am a divine *healing presence*, and I am an ambassador to and from the Spirit World. I help to ground spiritual reality in human life by translating spiritual energies and principals into a usable form of energy for my fellow human beings. Over the last twenty-two years, I have helped thousands of clients recover their good health and vitality. My clients refer to me as their "healer." I am more comfortable with the term "healing presence."

However, my past has been most ordinary. My upbringing in Germany was a childhood experience that held no promise of greatness or unique individuality in any way. On the contrary, I am sure that, if you knew the traumatic and emotionally violent details of my childhood, most of you would certainly commit me to failure. My parents were born before the Second World War and grew into their teens during the course of this gruesome tragedy. Severely traumatized by the experience, they had no psychological help to process the resulting fear, helplessness, and guilt. The devastation of this terrible war dismantled every aspect of my parents' lives. In order to cope, they froze their feeling bodies and remained in survival. With their emotional bodies numbed and curtailed in their expressions, they were unable to express affection and love. I don't remember ever being held, hugged, or caressed by my mother. A single kiss to my cheek from my mother was the sum total of affection that I am now able to recall.

My mother's emotional state would oscillate from sullen self-victimization to anger and blame, followed by hopeless dejection. Born as an extremely sensitive empath, I suffered my mother's pain and my dad's helplessness. Mostly, I lived in fear of my mother's painful emotions, which made me recoil from her, creating a physical and emotional distance between us that never lifted while she was alive. I lived in fear of her daily verbal attacks, a situation that never abated and continued until I decided to leave my parents' household shortly after my sixteenth birthday. I left with my father's secret consent to rent a small apartment on my own in the next town over. I am sure my dad did it as much for me as for himself, to get some peace from the relentless verbal attacks launched by my mother in my direction. Needless to say, I was way too young to be on my own. But I managed and thrived ... in the end.

Of course there is more, and I will give you a more detailed look inside my past as I go along writing this book, as it may be important to relate parts of my story to make a point or to bring about deeper understanding. But to begin with, I want to let you know that I was not born special, meaning under "special circumstances." Like most of you, I had a difficult past and many obstacles to overcome. I had no idea that life, my life, could be fun and fulfilling. It took me many years of shedding layers of pain and tears to get here. But I know firsthand that it can be done. I did it by following my inner heart's dream, my heart flame, as I was led by my heart's desire into freedom and enjoyment of the creation that is my life.

What is most extraordinary is my ability to heal and to advance myself energetically by making positive changes to my aura at will. I have developed this skill naturally but consciously over the last two decades. At first I was not aware of the fact that I was doing something revolutionary. I thought all healing science students were practicing self-healing like I was. In this private, intimate practice, I learned to regulate my energetic system, through the seven layers of my aura, positively affecting and improving all physical functioning. I have healed my knees and wrists after a painful condition following a yoga injury, healed my kidneys and bladder from chronic pain and infections, and cleared my large intestine from diverticulitis and my skin from a severe case of dermatitis (just to name a few). I have also healed my right arm and shoulder from a painful physical injury after a fall that left me unable to use my right arm. I have successfully dealt with depression and transformed long-lasting emotional despair into joy and passion for life.

I have done so with the help of my multidimensional support team (MDST).

My work as a healing presence is made possible by a continuing and evolving relationship with the extremely helpful, supportive light beings that make up my MDST. Over time, together, we have developed a sacred and mutual relationship that serves the greater good of all. The assistance and support of the beings on my team are instrumental in helping to heal the aura upon request. Its through these beings loving presence and supportive guidance that I have claimed myself as *who I am*. I am still amazed and immensely grateful that this gift has been bestowed on my presence to enjoy and share. It is my ability to communicate effectively with multidimensional reality and the resulting healing gift that lends authority to my voice. It was, in part, at the urging of my MDST that I wrote this book. This message of freedom, healing and spiritual cocreation wants to be known and is given with some urgency. Now more than ever, we need this universally intelligent input, the voice for elegant and practical solutions to serve the greater good for all.

Being able to heal ourselves is our innate birthright as human beings. But we have to claim it as such and make it *our choice*! It is by right action and diligent practice that we claim authority over our innate birthright to realize it in the here and now.

We are all creative beings of God. Look around you—all that

we see, excluding nature of course, is man-made. Most of what we use and enjoy has been conceived and created by human beings. We fly the skies, venture to the moon, and drive fantastic automobiles. Our communication devices are all but part of us. In light of that, what then makes us question our ability to heal ourselves? In my view, it is just another creative undertaking—an undertaking to which I have dedicated my life.

Even when I was a young girl, I could not fully accept that a doctor could know more about the insides of my body than I knew. I thought, *My body is mine. And I should know what is going on in my body—better than anyone*. It was the only thing that made sense to me. Somehow I knew that it was possible to self-govern my body and health. I remember looking at my hands and fingers, contemplating the end of my fingertips as a final boundary of my being. I asked myself, "Do I end here at my fingertips?" I actually spent quite a bit of time on that inquiry. Turns out, I don't. And neither do you. You don't end at your fingertips. This is what I find to be true: We are human beings, flesh and physical, as we are spirit, subtle energy and divine.

We are all made of God's creative energy. Your individual purpose is already encoded in your energetic body, and your longing is the key to the fulfillment of your purpose. Heart flame healing is your activated passion—activated by listening deeply to your inner heart's dream and making it your prime directive. Provided we choose our God presence, adhering to the highest aspect of who we can be, we are then guided by universal intelligence, upon request. Universal principals and commands are available for healing and the creation of positive reality in service for *the greater good of all*. And it is to this end that I have written *Heart Flame Healing*.

A little clarification is needed about my relationship with and understanding of God and how I use the term "God" in this book. It is my experience and understanding that we are, in fact guided by a higher universal intelligence—available to us for the asking. I am not affiliated with any kind of religion. Nor do I believe in a God as a supreme leader who judges us and sends us to hell or heaven. It is my current understanding that we are all participating in creating our individual and collective reality and that we are all part of that divine creative energy. This creative energy is, in fact, our birthright. We are part of that divine God consciousness, and it is up to us—to each individual—to participate uniquely in our own right to create what we so desire in our own lives and collectively. We are, you are, *I am life!* We are conscious, breathing life itself!

There is wisdom and intelligence to be tapped into as this life that we are, and that wisdom and intelligence is even beyond science. One can tap into spiritual reality by exploring and understanding one's own aura. Your energetic light body holds the key to fully understanding the body, mind, and soul connection and moving you into the wholeness that is your chosen life. I see and experience (my team) the light beings; these ascended masters, deities, and angels are an integral part of this universal wisdom and intelligence. Though they are not organized in physical reality, they assist physical reality from the subtle energetic spiritual dimension, with their accumulated goodwill, wisdom, and intelligence. They are, in fact, serving the greater good for all.

It is my promise that this manuscript will be a direct transmission, aided by divine universal intelligence, to help you establish a lasting and healing connection with your spirit body, the aura, and your chakra system. I will show you how you can connect through your aura to your divine spiritual heritage and, hence, be able to access your spiritual multidimensional guidance team to help you live the life of your choice. This book is, in fact, an invitation to begin a cocreative process with spiritual reality if you make this your choice.

I invite you to come along with me and venture into the layers of your aura and your chakra system. Learn how to heal your aura, your heart, your body, and your life by practicing easy-to-learn healing skills like the art of receiving, being gentle, harmonizing, allowing, and choosing to live in positive reality.

Your sacred longing is real, and it does have a purpose in and of itself. Have the courage to feel it, to listen to it, and to honor its presence in your life. It will show you the way to the fulfillment of your life. Your longing is designed to do exactly that, as it is the living road sign to the fulfillment of your inner heart's dream.

How to Read This Book

Dear reader, it is my hope that, by reading this book, you'll be inspired to claim your unique and creative energy to fully manifest your heart's desire and longing. *Heart Flame Healing* (*HFH*) was written under divine guidance in an organic way in order to enable optimal learning. I recommend that you read it first from beginning to end and perhaps make notes of the questions that arise. Then go back and read it again, in part, or the whole thing, as you are drawn to certain parts of it. Finally, use *HFH* as a reference. Most of your questions will probably be answered the second time around. Other questions will be answered in time. This book is an accumulation of many years of practical knowledge; just as your aura has layers, *HFH* also has layers. And as with any new knowledge, there is a learning curve. Allow for it.

Let this be your adventure in discovering the four aspects of your human being: Gain a new appreciation for your *physical body*; get to know and experience your *aura and chakra system*; learn to live from your *hara*; and radiate your *core star* presence. These four human dimensions—(1) the physical body, (2) the aura and chakra system, (3) your hara, and (4) your core star presence—are already present within you and supporting you in your highest good.

Here in the preface and in the introduction, I share some of my personal story and the reasons for writing this book. I hope my story will inspire your courage to dive deeply into your own longing—no matter what came before.

Part One

This first part consists of chapters 1 through 6. Here, I discuss the basics of the aura, the chakra system, the hara line, and the core star dimension, as well as the multidimensional support team (MDST).

In chapter 1, I present the healing skills—connecting with your inner heart's dream and allowing, harmonizing, and energizing your intention. Practicing them will support you immediately in your quest and in your daily life. As you practice, say statements out loud whenever you can. In time, you'll notice how they affect your body and your energy as you speak the statements.

Chapter 2 gives an overview of the aura, chakra system, hara, and core star dimension.

Chapter 3 is all about the first chakra. As it is the foundation for your physical health and well-being, I have devoted a whole chapter to it. It covers important facets of first chakra health, such as how walking, resting, and past life longing can influence the health of your first chakra.

One of my teachers, Barbara Ann Brennan, said in one of her lectures that all disease in some way relates back to a distorted first chakra. I do agree with her.

In chapter 4, we'll explore in more depth the aura and chakra system. Building on the material from the overview, it will help you to absorb the material in more detail.

In chapter 5, you'll learn about the art of resting and receiving, which are important healing skills to begin practicing right away.

Chapter 6 explores in depth the multidimensional support team (MDST), what it is, and how to begin to form a lasting connection. In this chapter, I share quite a bit of my own story. Hopefully, it will inspire you to recognize your own team and the generous beings that are already supporting you. To help cultivate your relationship with your divine friends, the previous chapter, five, serves to prepare your body and mind to better receive those subtle messages from your already existing team. Enjoy the process!

Part Two

In part two, we will take a look at how other practices can add wholeness to your life and support your endeavor of manifesting your longing.

Chapter 7 highlights the opportunity of being awake in the early morning hours, presenting an invitation to give up lament over lost sleep in favor of moving into positive reality. This chapter is an example of how positive reality orientation can turn a perceived negative into the ultimate opportunity to claim and fulfill your longing.

Chapter 8 clarifies past-life phenomenon and how it can relate to our present-day suffering or longing. Unfinished and unforgiven material from the past tend to show up in difficult reoccurring emotions, physical pain, and limiting belief systems that keep us stuck in old ways. Forgiveness is key in healing past-life trauma. I have included a personal example of a past-life trauma being healed (on the spot) with forgiveness. If you are suffering from a chronic situation, this may be one of the most important chapters for you to read. Give yourself time to absorb and understand this chapter, especially if the information is new to you.

Chapter 9 is all about "merging"; it discusses what merging is, the different types of merging, and how to unmerge. For many of you, this concept of merging in terms of healing is going to be new to you. But you'll quickly recognize how merging has or is affecting you on a daily basis. Sensitive individuals who are unfamiliar with the workings of merging might have a few aha moments. Practice the healing statements in this chapter. They are invaluable for unmerging and coming back to your own peace of mind.

Chapter 10 explores the importance, value, and gifts of a daily meditation practice, which is an essential ingredient in self-healing, and offers support in unmerging. Enough said! Please enjoy this chapter and start right away.

In chapter 11, we'll take a look at your outer domain, the house that you live in, which is your greater body. Just as old habitual patterns can hold us back and keep us from moving forward, a cluttered home may drain your energy and keep you stuck in old ways. Take inspiration from this chapter to clean out the old to make space for the adventure of your new life.

Chapter 12 is about putting it all together with your personal practice. Organized in a natural flow, this chapter matches chakras to the days of the week so that, each day, you'll focus on a different chakra to deepen your knowledge with practice over time. Much of this information I have shared with you is energetic information, meaning you'll much better understand it when you can feel and sense it in your body and your life. This will take time and repetition, especially if most of this information is new to you. Intellectual learning is not going to suffice; you'll have to practice regularly to claim the healing skills for yourself. Practice with joy and playfulness, and you'll elevate it into an art. Have fun!

I hope that my epilogue will additionally inspire you to reach for your dream, no matter what came before or how long it takes.

Introduction

I was in my late teens, perhaps nineteen, walking home from the Frankfurt Haubt Bahnhof train station. It was a typical German afternoon in late spring, gray skies hanging low, overcast; the dreariness mimicked the absence of joy I felt inside my heart and all around me. Suddenly, I was present to disconnection, a lack of meaning to all the life bustling around me. For the first time in my life, I heard this voice; it wasn't so much in my head, but rather, it seemed to come from my heart and my whole body: *I am not happy, not here, not like this!*

I know now that this was the voice of longing, from my future self, waiting to come alive. It rung true, as it knew of a possibility, a happiness outside of my current circumstances. Once distinguished and heard, it was like a bell that kept on ringing in the background, changing the vibration and direction of my life.

By the end of that year, I was on a plane, polishing my English skills while listening to my Berlitz tapes as I made the transatlantic crossing, on my way to a new life in the United States of America.

Nine years later, the voice of my future self sounded of again, announcing a change in the direction of my life. And indeed it was needed. Standing in front of my bedroom mirror in a flat that I shared with four other hard-partying Australian housemates, I listened as the voice of truth silently pointed out the errors of my ways. I was in Paddington in Sydney, Australia, on a sabbatical from my life in California, where I had been building a practice as a massage therapist. After years of touching people to relieve their pain, overcome with disillusion and compassion fatigue, I had decided on this trip as a soul-searching adventure. Feeling empty, alone, and without a clear purpose, I was hoping to find myself; a sense of belonging; and, most of all, love. But I could see now that I had been looking in all the wrong places. As I contemplated my image, the mirror reflected a future I did not want. Suddenly it was clear to me that, if I kept going in the same direction of my current default setting, I would surely end up in the gutter. For all practical purposes, I was touching the bottom of the barrel. Living a life of debauchery and partying, I was consuming a steady diet of recreational drugs, cigarettes, and alcohol, and without exercise. I had lost my way, rather than finding it. Trying to escape my pain with unsavory and sometimes dangerous indulgences, I had bankrupted myself and obliterated the wholesomeness of my youth. Here I was at the edge of my existence, a sad pair of eyes looking back at me, weary, hopeless, scared, and dreading the consequences of my reckless behavior. This was not who I wanted to be! I knew better!

Desperate to be alive and missing my vibrant wholesome self, I made an SOS call to a trusted friend back in the States. While I was, indeed, alarmed by what I had seen in the mirror—a jaundiced-looking face revealing traces of recreational drug abuse and a general lack of self-care—something else inside of me moved into action. An inner drive, a strong desire to be healthy and whole again, a need to be on the right path and to fulfill my life's purpose took over and guided my actions.

While on the phone with my friend Glen in the United States, I remembered someone had mentioned a natural detox place near San Diego in California. I asked Glen to locate and research that place I had heard about.

Glen called me back the very next day with his findings. The Ann Wickmore Optimum Health Institute in San Diego was exactly what I needed. It offered an all raw food healing and detox program. I decided to return to the States and booked myself in for the entire three-week program. Opening myself to an invaluable life-changing healing experience, I received a priceless practical education, while healing myself naturally with raw foods—a practice and lifestyle that still supports my health and vibrant energy to this day.

My stay at the Optimum Health Institute turned out to be an inspiring rejuvenation. Fueled by vibrant energy provided by the Wickmore raw life food protocol, my life force increased, helping me to turn my life around. As I continued to study natural healing methods, connecting with others of like mind, I formed alliances, began to create workshops, and started teaching about the healing powers of natural foods.

Soon after, I signed on with a new friend. A charismatic woman and a seasoned marriage and family child therapist with a private practice, who had invented an emotional clearing process. She took me on as a protégée to learn her process.

Marge invited me into a business partnership, which ultimately promised more than it could deliver. I know now that it was based on a half-baked concept and was doomed to fail as what it was. Nevertheless, it seemed like a good idea at the time. Swayed by my soon-to-be business partner's enthusiasm and her convincing enrollment conversation, I jumped on board this leaky vessel. The business partnership with Marge soon failed, faltering not long after its launch.

Turns out it was a pie in the sky—my pie-in-the-sky experience! As the disillusion of this failed venture hit home, a storm brewed, unhinging the now strained partnership.

The voice of undeniable truth spoke to me for the third time. I was now thirty-four years old, and my life, once again, came crashing down in a single swoop. My business partner Marge, in the clutches of an emotional upheaval, terminated our arrangement, effective immediately. This left me homeless, without a car or an office in which to see my clients, a situation that threatened to have me penniless within weeks.

The day of our parting argument, I was standing in the bathroom. As I dried my hands, I looked up to the mirror and into the dark of my eyes. I was surprised by my voice, speaking to my image as earnestly and directly as if another person was addressing me from the inside. I spoke without a thought. "I want to know my God self!"

Looking down at my hands, now holding on to the sink, I was puzzled over this strong comment that had escaped my mouth seemingly out of nowhere. Testing, I looked up again into my eyes, and the same sentence came out of my mouth. It was my own voice but the voice of my *new* self—yet to be born. Still, it was firm and true. "I want to know my God self!"

Part of me woke right then and there, feeling a sense of relief over hearing it, the voice of my true self. This voice was clear, confident, and calm. There was no second-guessing. I instinctively knew I could trust this voice and that it would guide me where I needed to go.

Years passed before I fully understood what had happened in that moment. But every time I thought about it, I knew this was truth. Hence, I claimed my voice of guidance for good.

It was the voice of longing, of my inner heart's dream to live and fulfill the purpose of my life. I made the choice to follow the highest directive and discovered ultimate creativity in the voice of my God self—or what I call now my *divine genius of God*. From that moment on, everything changed in my life. New doors opened, and I stepped through.

What I found exceeded my expectations. Step by step, I was guided to a life that I knew I had dreamed up. I am now living my inner heart's dream, true to my longing and fulfilling the promise of my life.

My First Healing Skills: Asking for Help and Appreciation

So here I was as I began to write *HFH*, on the threshold of fulfilling yet another longing of mine. At this point, I didn't really know how to write a book. But that was not going to deter me from writing my book and having it published. I was committed to seeing it through. And to do so, I enlisted the help of my multidimensional support team. Feeling unsure about the results of my first week of writing, I asked my MDST for a dream that would let me know I was on the right track.

That following morning before waking, I had a dream. I was in the cellar of a house, a big house like a mansion. I knew the house was quite substantial, given that it had an underground garage. I found myself standing near a fantastic-looking race car. It looked like a Formula One race car, and I knew it was mine to drive. I remembered communicating with an invisible presence, telling it and myself that I knew how to get it out of here (the underground garage) because I had gotten it in here. I saw myself getting in the car. Then the dream shifted, and I was watching another scene. Two people were coming onto a stage to sing. One had a guitar. Obviously, he could sing and was leading the other, who was new to this and sang along in an unskilled, awkward way but enthusiastically. When I awoke, I knew that the car was mine; it was the book inside of me, and it was mine to drive. I could take it out on the open road of the world and share this knowledge of healing oneself with the assistance of divine intelligence, a skill that is available to everyone for the asking.

I now felt confident in my ability. I got it inside of me. Hence, I knew that I would get it out of the garage. What would be the point of having all this useful information, symbolized by this beautiful race car, and not sharing it on the open road of life? The stage dream confirmed that, yes, I was new to this, and I didn't know how to do it, but I was willing to be mentored, to be shown the way. Enthusiasm was key. I had my reassurance that I was on the right track. Thank you to my wonderful supportive MDST.

And thank you, my dear friend, the reader. *You* were here with me from the beginning of the process. I could feel your longing too, inside my own. This is what made me return to the page, keeping with the rhythm of writing. Thank you for your presence!

Part One

Chapter 1

The Heart Flame

The heart has its reasons which reason knows nothing of.

—Blaise Pascal

So, my dear friend, let's dive right in, shall we? Why did you pick up this book? What is it that you are looking for? Perhaps you are guided by your heart flame, the spiritual fire burning in your heart of hearts, with a strong desire to fulfill aspects of your life that are waiting to be discovered. This is a good place to start—right here, exactly as you are. There is no need to change anything. Feel yourself as you are. Deep in your heart, what is your longing and what is the feeling that cannot be denied?

Your inner heart's dream (IHD) is a message from your soul and a road map to fulfillment. It always guides you in the right direction, without fail. The journey taken may not go in a straight line—it seldom does—but it will get you there. If you are alive, you have a longing, a desire to fulfill. Some may call it a goal, which can be a lesser expression of your longing. You may know what it is, or you may not. If you are not fully in touch with your longing, you might be envious of another who has what you so desire.

For example, you may harbor a still shrouded longing (you're not fully aware of its existence, but it's still submerged in the unconscious) to own your own business. Every time you come across a certain venue (one that reminds you of your own longing) you might be gripped by a sense of envy. Perhaps you may even be critical of how the venue is run, thinking that you most certainly would do a better job. This is a more negative or shrouded expression of your inner heart's dream. Usually the shrouding is accompanied by a closed heart chakra. The hallmark of a closed heart chakra is criticism, either of yourself or of others. So if you are looking for your longing, look also in the places where you are most critical. It might give you a clue and provide an unexpected opening.

Your IHD is the ultimate promise that your life holds; it's that which you dream to be, either consciously or unconsciously. If you are ill, you are sure to desire good health so you can go on with the business of living. The illness itself can be part of the journey to the fulfillment of your inner heart's dream.

The IHD is part of the hara, which is an energetic organization in the form of a living line of light inside the centerline of your body. A level deeper than the aura, the hara supports your purpose for this life in what is called the hara line. The hara line, if it is not broken, goes straight through your bones. Rising up from the center of the earth, it goes through the center of the bones in the legs, coming together in the lower pelvis above the pubic bone and below the belly button as a golden liquid fireball of creative energy, also called the tan tien. The tan tien is in direct relationship to the soul seat in the upper chest, where your longing for the manifestation of your IHD resides. From here, the hara line reaches up and out of the body, culminating at about a foot to a foot and a half above the head in what is called the ID point; this forms a personal connection to God, or the source of all.

The inner heart's dream resides in your upper chest. Yes, it does have a physical home; it inhabits the energetic place of your thymus gland. We tend to put our hands up to this tender place when we speak about what really matters to us. Next time you have an intimate conversation with someone, notice his or her hands and how they move in relationship to what matters to the person most. Even if you already feel you know your inner heart's dream, give this next exercise a try.

Healing Skill: Connecting with Your Inner Heart's Dream or Longing

Now, in order to connect with your inner heart's dream, be still and feel what really matters to you right now. What can't you do without and what would make you feel sad if this thing did not come to pass? For instance, without this sacred work of mine and, at this point, without my book, I would feel a tremendous loss. Even if I had all the money in this world, I would still want to help others and spread the knowledge of the healing power of the human aura and the sacred longing of the inner heart's dream.

What are you burning for or lusting after? If you have connected with something at my prompting, you can be sure that it is your inner heart's dream, pulsing forward with the desire to fulfill your life.

At times, in some individuals, the IHD might be shrouded, frozen, or hidden because life has demanded their attention elsewhere. You may have had to spend time taking care of a sick loved one and forgotten about yourself for a while. Or you might have been brought up to believe that there is no such thing as an inner heart's dream or longing to fulfill. If you were raised in an environment where goal setting and accomplishments took precedence over nurturing and encouraging aspects of your unique individuality, then you may have a more challenging time recognizing your inner heart's dream. Don't let yourself be discouraged if you encounter feelings of emptiness accompanied by frustration. If this is the case, your best bet is to see what gives you joy and makes you feel alive. If you still come up short, allow yourself to live with these questions: What gives you life and joy? What draws you in and lights you up?

Yes, everyone has an IHD. It lives within your upper chest in the location of your sternum. Even if you don't feel anything, you still have an inner heart's dream. It may not be pulsing with aliveness if it is frozen and buried deep inside of you. How, then, will you find it? Look for the discomfort, frustration, or pain in your life. Ask yourself where this discomfort resides. Is it physical, emotional, or mental? Perhaps it's all of the above. Don't be afraid; you'll be okay. Feel the sensation, breathe into it, allow it to be there, and give it room to exist. Let this awareness show you the way.

You may have already fulfilled one or more aspects of your inner heart's dream. For example, let's say that one of your deep longings as a young adult was to be a parent and that this yearning has been fulfilled, as your children are grown and have left home to follow their own dreams. You might be struggling to reconnect with your inner heart's dream. This can be a particularly challenging time for men and women who loved being parents above all else. This is the transitioning of the empty-nest syndrome. But don't worry; if you connected with it once, you will again, provided you make doing so your choice.

Healing Skill: The Void and Making It Your Choice

Even if you find yourself in a momentary void—a feeling of emptiness and not knowing what is next—relax; you are in the perfect place. Allow yourself to feel it. It's okay to feel the emptiness. By making the void your choice, you assume authority over your creative process in all aspects of the manifestation of your IHD. Allow the deep, dark, fertile ground to nurture that ever-so-tiny seed of longing so your creative expression can bloom and come alive.

Why would you choose the void if what you really want is to connect with your longing? The void is a space of infinite possibility. In positive reality, it is the pure goodness of empty space. It is a potent and fertile ground for your creative spark to enter and light up the dark. In the void is a readiness—a waiting; a wanting; and, ideally, a peaceful nurturing of the IHD in that fertile ground. Be willing to chop wood and carry water until the next creative impulse arises to carry you forward again. Think of a perennial flower bulb, one that bloomed last year and has been underground all winter long. Resting in the earth and waiting for the rays of the sun to warm the ground, the bulb lies dormant until finally in the spring a new leaf sprouts. Still it remains under the ground, but soon it will see the light of the day. The void is like that; the dark fertile earth is holding the seed of your next creation, preparing it to sprout. The sprouting of this new leaf will most likely have you reaching out to the world to make contact with like-minded people or seeking a new experience, moving your longing forward and making it real.

When you find yourself in a void space, it may seem that all (outer) forward movement has come to a halt. There may also be a feeling of boredom or stagnation. Given voice, a positive inner relationship to being in the void would say, "I am at a plateau, resting to gather new creative energy and inspiration to move forward once again on the next wave of a new creative impulse." The next creative impulse, that spark of inspiration and a movement forward will then come naturally out of enough rest and an activity that supports your overall well-being. Do the things that "work" in your life with care and trust in the knowledge that the creative tide will turn once again, when enough energy has been gathered deep inside your being.

The void space is a perfect time to solidify and integrate new knowledge and good habits of self-care, like gardening, deepening your practice of yoga, or perfecting your healthy food preparation into a culinary art. Cleaning up your personal space at this time can work wonders to make room for a new wave of creative energy; this clears out the old and makes space for the new. In this time of the void, "chopping wood and carrying water" can offer wide-ranging benefits, if one surrenders to it, as positive intention has the power to elevate an ordinary chore into an art.

A negative orientation to the void space would be a feeling of being stuck or going backward into outdated habits or negative self-talk. One might suffer critical and self-defeating inner commentary, like, "It's all over now," or, "It doesn't matter anyway," or, "What's the use?"

To distract oneself from the emptiness inside, one may be tempted to indulge in too much food and drink, too many movies, online shopping, endlessly scrolling through Facebook or Instagram, or browsing the internet.

Know that, if you are surrendering consciously to the void space, the forward movement of the new creative impulse will come naturally in its own time. Be patient and stay present even to the simple tasks of ordinary living. Most importantly, don't judge anything. Be curious as to what draws your attention and what pulls you into action.

The void can be a scary place because it may seem like the end of something, rather than a beginning of something new and beautiful. I have been in the void so many times that I had to make friends with it. Now I know, that when the void arrives, a new creative energy is ahead. But like everyone else who has encountered this mysterious place before, I have struggled. In fact, I went through a void period only a few weeks before beginning this manuscript.

I was living in the fulfillment of my inner heart's dream, enjoying my freedom as an artist of life and a successful healer. Then in the twelfth year of my healing practice, I arrived at a place of divine dissatisfaction. At first I kept this uncomfortable feeling at bay by redoing my apartment, updating my wardrobe, going hiking or out for dinner with friends, and watching movies. In the background, a wave of unfulfilled desire began to squeeze me from the inside, making me increasingly more uncomfortable every day. In my free time, my enjoyment of watching a movie diminished, online clothing boutiques seemed to sap my energy, and even sleeping became a restless event. I watched myself slide into panic at having too much time alone on a weekend and noticed a desire to overindulge. My treasured inner peace was eluding me. Eventually, I decided to fully let myself feel what was going on, and I once again entered the void by consciously choosing it. I allowed it and made it my choice. I even announced it to my most trusted friends and asked for their support, which helped a lot to be at peace with it.

I spent a few days feeling the discomfort of the empty space of the void and found that my longing, my inner heart's dream, was to write my book. I had been here before when I had started to write and then stopped. Afraid to have yet another unfinished version, I knew I had to finish it this time and see it through. I felt that I would be deeply sad if it did not come to pass. And whose fault would it be? I knew I could not pass this off as a result of early childhood trauma anymore. Been there, done that! *Just let it go*, I told myself. *It's too much trouble. I don't know how to do it.*

I imagined myself without my book. By mentally and emotionally going down that road, I saw that, in the end, I would have no choice but to write it. Without my book, a piece of myself was going to be missing. I would not be happy without the finished version of my book.

Wherever you find yourself right now, if you are already connected and know what your inner heart's dream is, that is wonderful. Harmonize with it. If you don't know what it is or how to find it, know that it is already inside of you, waiting to be discovered. How exciting!

Your IHD has everything to do with your purpose or purposes in life. If you desire purpose, then you have one. Your first step might be to feel the desire to have a purposeful life. This desire may come out of a feeling of emptiness. If emptiness is there, honor the space itself without making it wrong. Feel it deeply without defense. Don't move to fill it. Be with it and make peace with it. Allow it! It is your friend. Be brave and feel the void.

Longing Meditation

Do this meditation a few days in a row to give yourself space to feel into different aspects of your longing.

- Choose a location to sit for ten minutes.
- Get comfortable with a straight back (if you can).
- Focus on your natural flow of breath.
- Feel into the space of your upper chest, your sternum.
- What do you feel here in this tender place?
- What wants to come alive?
- What is your great longing right now?
- Whatever you encounter, say, "I allow it!"

Healing Skill: Harmonizing

Harmonizing is a wonderful life skill. It works like magic. By harmonizing with a project or a person, you come into positive relationship with it or with him or her, aligning with the highest possibilities of that project or person. The practice of harmonizing clears away most interference and obstacles from the get-go. It turns challenges into opportunities and opens doors that otherwise might be missed. When you harmonize with your project, you are automatically aligning with those individuals in support of your project, making it easy for you to recognize each other and meet up in your united purpose.

How do you harmonize with a person or a project? You make it *your choice* to be in harmony with that person or project. It is by saying, doing, and being it that you come into harmony with your choice. It is as simple as that. It works best if you take a little time each day to focus on positive alignment with your inner heart's desire.

Harmonizing

- Decide what or who you want to harmonize with.
- Then say, "It is my choice to harmonize with [name the person or thing you wish to harmonize with]. That is my choice and thank you!"
- Hold yourself to it, meaning, if you are harmonizing with a particular person, resist a mental argument in your own head with that person. Keep saying, "It is my choice to harmonize with [name the person or thing you wish to harmonize with], and that is my choice."
- If you harmonize with a project, don't doubt your success. Be in positive relationship with the desired outcome.

An Example of Harmonizing

During the writing of this book, to prepare myself for the task of writing, I sat and harmonized with the finished book project at the beginning of every day for five minutes. This meant that I came into positive relationship with it. First, I harmonized with my IHD, my longing for the book and all that it means to me. Then I harmonized with the finished project. Feeling and seeing *Heart Flame Healing* completed, I came into positive relationship every step of the way to completion. I saw the cover image, noticed the book's compact size, and felt the quality of the paper and the weight of the finished book in my hands. As I thumbed mentally through the pages, I imagined the people who would read and benefit from my book. I harmonized with them too. I was in positive relationship with my project and all that was involved.

Your inner heart's dream or heart's desire is in ultimate alignment with your purpose here. It will guide you to the fulfillment of your purpose.

Healing Skill: Allowing

If you are feeling frustration or an emotional reaction in relationship to your IHD because you can't connect with it or you are afraid to fully feel it because you don't know how to fulfill it, "allow it." Give yourself permission to feel your discomfort or unease. In other words, don't fight it or leave the premises. Give yourself the space to feel and be with what is going on. Physically notice where you have a sensation in your body when focusing on your longing. Ask yourself, "What is the emotion here?" Mentally examine the judgments that arise. What are your personal thoughts on your longing?

By allowing what is, the longing underneath it all will offer up valuable information, helping to clear the way for the next step in the fulfillment of your IHD. It is natural to feel frustrated over that which we have not yet moved to fulfill. Emotional pain may be present itself, as you are grieving missed opportunities. And your ego mind may be telling you that it is futile to even attempt to fulfill your inner heart's dream. Let it be. These are old voices. Say, "Thank you for sharing, but this is a new chapter of my life." Allow it all. Don't defend against the inner commentary. In fact, invite it and say, "Tell me more." Then listen and repeat until you get more familiar with the true feelings in your upper chest. You are treasure hunting for the holy grail of your life. It's a worthwhile cause.

As we move along the path of heart flame healing, I'll refer repeatedly to the command, "Allow it!" But why? Our natural inclination when faced with discomfort, frustration, or pain is to move away from it as quickly as we can. Grab an aspirin to alleviate our headache. Sugar and alcohol are also widely abused to cope and self-medicate when we encounter these bumps in the road.

To be sure, I am not talking about unbearable pain here. Hopefully we all know when to seek out help for pain that is truly alarming. I am talking about minor pains or sensations from your physical-emotional feedback system that indicate a course correction is needed. Discomfort can arise when we are prompted to change by a physical, emotional, or mental manifestation. Two examples are the uncomfortable feeling of an emotion (that wants to clear) rising in the body before it is fully conscious or the intuitive knowing that a relationship is about to change or come to an end.

It is by *allowing* the discomfort first that we can get inside the issue, in order to feel it out. When you say, "I allow it," you are stating, "I am here. I am not vacating the premises. I am willing to be a witness to what is going on here." Then, you are present to the sensation without defense allowing the change to occur. Allowing is a healing skill that is refined over time. Practicing this healing skill can move you into greater freedom and away from potentially harmful reactionary behavior.

I introduced a client to the concept of allowing during a healing session. When she came back the next time, she told me that it had indeed given her a newfound freedom in her life. She realized that she did not have to go into an automatic defense reaction because someone was negative or vented anger. She could now, silently, allow it! Allowing something also gives you space from it; it helps you differentiate and stay in your own experience. Chances are, when you "allow it," you stay grounded and on target.

Healing Skill: Energizing Your Intention

When embarking on a new creative adventure, old routines may not be sufficient to help facilitate a juicy creative flow. Adding a physical routine can help to energize your intention.

For example, adding a writing routine is a challenge that requires me to organize my life in more precise ways. If I sit for too long, I get the feeling of being all tangled up. Words won't come out in a cohesive or succinct way to form a sentence that makes sense. I feel stuck and get frustrated. To help me stay on track with my writing project, I energize my intention by increasing my physical practice. I decide on more yoga and hiking to fuel the fire in my belly and for a healthy dose of oxygen to my brain.

What do you need to do to energize your intention?

What would be fun for you?

The Power of Thank You: A Healing Skill

*If the only prayer you ever say in your whole
life is "thank you," that would suffice.*

—Meister Eckhart

I am sure many of you have heard about the late Dr. Masaru Emoto, author of *The Hidden Messages in Water*. If you are not familiar with Dr. Masaru or his work, it will be well worth your time to find out about him. His research and messages about water are nothing less than astonishing.

In his work, he clearly demonstrates the effect language has on the structure of water crystals. Dr. Masaru took water samples that had been prayed over, talked to, or treated with messages that were taped to the container holding the water. He then froze the sample and took photographs of the frozen crystals. The photos show clearly that the structure of water is responsive to language and intent. The crystals of the water that had been treated with messages of kindness and thanks were beautifully formed and complete, but the water crystals that had been exposed to a message of hate were clearly incoherent and distorted. When you see the photos of the water crystals that had been exposed to "Thank you," you'll never again underestimate the power of those two little words.

Given the fact that our physical bodies are mostly water, Dr. Masaru's message is compelling and speaks for loving kindness as a healing skill. Clearly, the quality of our inner conversation can make us whole or break us down. So drink up that good water and talk kindly to yourself and others.

Chapter 2

An Overview of the Aura, the Chakra System, the Hara Line, and the Core Star Dimension

Keeping my inner eyes and mind open, I began to see and feel the structures that make up the chakras, including the distortions that hold so much human suffering in place.

—Karin Inana

Now I would like to introduce to you the wonderful and exciting world of your aura and chakra system, the hara, the core star, and your multidimensional support team.

Your aura is your subtle energy body, a network made up of lines of light that includes the chakras. It holds and supports your physical body inside a living blueprint. In fact, the aura is a vital part of being alive in this human body, as the aura is the go-between, linking the spirit and anchoring it to the human body. Without the aura, we have no life. At the time of our death, with the conclusion of the last breath, the aura (what is left of it, because the lower levels of the aura disintegrate in the dying process) lifts out of the physical and moves into the unseen spiritual realm. The aura is a dynamic, complex, and conscious system that holds memory even beyond this life. This pulsing, living, and layered blueprint nurtures our human being with spiritual intelligence and loving vibrations. When healthy, it informs, heals, and can evolve all aspects of human life, including physical, emotional, mental, and spiritual aspects. The aura provides a means of staying vitally connected to universal intelligence and the sacred source of all.

The chakra system is a vital part of the aura. In fact, the chakras are the details of the aura. Chakras are energetic structures made up of lines of light, forming the spinning vortices that regulate the human aura. All chakras are connected through a complex network of lines of light in the aura. There are seven major chakras and seven layers to the human aura, and each chakra has also seven layers. By studying the human aura, we open to a vast body of knowledge that inevitably carries us into the spiritual dimensions.

There is no substitute for direct experience. So much is written about the aura and the chakras, and I encourage you to gather all the information you need. But more importantly, I am inviting you to feel and sense into your own aura and chakra system, to discover for yourself the vast territory that opens before you as you enter into the exploration and experience of your personal multidimensional support system, your aura.

More than anything, this is how I acquired the unique body of knowledge that was imparted to me. I went directly, with the help of my MDST, into my own field. Keeping my inner eyes and mind open, I began to see and feel the structures that make up the chakras, including the distortions that hold so much human suffering in place. One by one, I was shown how to replace each one of those faulty structures with a new and upgraded version. I was taught how to release ancient past-life traumas from my body and consciousness. I learned about the healing power of forgiveness and how to enlist my multidimensional support team for the purpose of healing myself. With the help of my MDST, I was lifted out of the ordinary and into a state of previously unsurpassed health and well-being in all areas of my life. Leftover traumas from my early childhood upbringing that for so many years had cast a shadow over my life began to leave my body, clearing my mind and emotions. In many ways, I felt dark veils lifted one by one, revealing the creative, joyful vitality of my true essence. I claimed my birthright, accepting that I have the power to heal myself. This insight accelerated my learning about the human aura, specifically the healing of my own aura. With each session, I was guided and shown how to make positive changes to my aura and to improve my life.

Distortions in chakras are always related to past trauma and a resulting faulty belief system. When these traumas and resulting faulty belief systems are released, healed, and then replaced—by working specifically with the aura—a new and expanded life opportunity will usually open. This is similar to how an upgraded version of your phone or computer expands your possibilities.

At the time, I didn't know that I was receiving a most revolutionary way of healing myself and others. Step by step over the years, one self-healing session built upon another, until the picture completed itself. I now have all of the details, and I am able teach this extraordinary, elegant, and simple method to others. It is simple because it does not require anything outside of yourself and elegant because it enhances the experience of your essence, which is a lot of fun.

Your aura is your bioenergetic computer. Of course this is a metaphor. But, yes, it is the operating system of your spirit body, as the network of the aura bridges energetic spiritual reality with physical reality. It, therefore, allows for a new possibility of interaction between spiritual and physical reality—much like the personal computer expanded possibilities and opportunities in personal life and business. Getting intimate and personal with your aura can bring a new sense of freedom and wholeness to your life. Think of your body as your hardware, your aura as your operating system, and your chakras as your software. The hara is your internet server or web browser. Just as each software application has a specific function, each chakra has a unique function in your body and field.

Most of us tend to think of ourselves as separate units, in a

Newtonian way. We view the body as a mechanical, separately functioning biological entity—until we find out we are not so separate at all. When we live our life from the perspective of the aura, the hara, and the core star dimension, it takes us from an experience of Newtonian (separate) reality into quantum (everything is connected) reality. Suddenly, worlds open before us, and we are able to go where we could only dream of venturing before. We become fully creative beings of God, or good!

Your aura is your subtle energy body, holding and supporting your physical body inside a layered blueprint that nurtures the physical reality of your human being with spiritual intelligence and loving vibrations. Your aura helps to inform, heal, and evolve all aspects of human life, including physical, emotional, mental, and spiritual aspects. The aura provides a means of staying vitally connected to universal intelligence and the sacred source of all.

Through working with the human energy field or aura, we are able to form a cocreative, supportive, and healing relationship with our multidimensional support team, by which physical suffering can be greatly reduced and, in many cases, eliminated. Universal intelligence, or the intelligence of "life itself" gives us the means (with the help of our MDST) by which many ailments, which are rampant right now in human experience, can be addressed effectively with ease and grace.

I have had many clients go from complaining about exhaustion, depression, and digestive issues to being symptom free in a matter of weeks. Healing and relief was accomplished by working with their auras to restore optimum functioning. I begin with the client's first chakra, for grounding and restoring the body's natural ability to release trauma through the legs into the earth. The second chakra restructuring helps to release old emotions and to restart the rejuvenation process. Then, moving on to the heart chakra, restructuring helps clear past-life and relationship trauma. I also address other chakras as I am guided to the next energetic structure that holds the key to unlocking the optimum flow of life-force energy.

I avail myself, on a regular basis, of the divine healing services that are offered so generously by my MDST. After all these years, I am still amazed at the level of detail and depth that can be achieved with high-level healing at my request and command. I know that this is available to everyone as a skill and as an art to be mastered into *the art of self-healing*.

The aura is the bioenergetic field emanating from every living thing and being. The human aura can be seen and felt, especially by those who have knowledge about it and are trained to work with it. But the layperson can see the aura as well. Generally, we respond to the aura of others quite naturally. We may say that this person is dark or this one has a lot of light. We can see when our best friend is in love by the expression on her face. And we can also feel the aura by emanation or the "vibe" a person is giving off.

The aura is our sensitive energy body. With a trained or activated aura, we can see and feel beyond the normal human realm of perception. By reading this book, you are becoming more familiar with the aura. Chances are you'll be inspired and curious to look at others to see the clues, signs, and colors of their auras. At first it is like learning to speak another language, as repetition is needed to make a new concept stick. But over time and with practice, accessing and addressing your own aura is likely to become effortless and even second nature.

Higher sensory perception, or HSP, is the ability to see, feel, and sense beyond the normal realms. One can study HSP and go to school and train for it. But often the gift of sight, intuition, or direct knowing is bestowed on healers and shamans, as well as on the person next to you. In other words, anybody can have or acquire HSP, including you.

Give yourself permission to know, see, and feel your own aura. Right now, take a moment and feel your hands. Sit still for a few minutes and notice the feeling in and around your hands. Do you sense a cloud-like, warm energy around your hands, perhaps spiraling out of your palms? As you put your hands slowly together, not quite touching, what do you feel? Chances are, you are becoming aware of the subtle sensations of your aura around your hands. If you do this every day for a few minutes, more detail will reveal itself.

It is by first accepting and then accessing their HSP that healers and other sensitive beings can see, feel, or know, distortions in the human energy field. The aura is as alive as we are at any given moment. It has color and intelligence and holds memory beyond our conscious memory. The aura holds within itself the mystery and memory of who we have been in other lives, as in past lives.

The human aura contains the physical body and governs all of its functions through the pulsing living blueprint that it is. It is by way of the aura that the spirit being, or life force, that animates the physical body grounds itself and becomes physical. The aura allows for the creation of the body in physical reality by vibrating and holding the template, which is the blueprint for our whole being—physically, emotionally, mentally and spiritually.

The aura is made up in structures and layers, alternately with pulsing lines of light and a cloud-like substance that has color and flows freely when healthy. All seven layers are interconnected and in communication with each other, but each has a very specific function. The aura is the living temple for our multidimensional spirit being, making it possible for our spirit being to become and stay in physical reality. One could say that the aura is more alive than is our physical body. When we die, we transition out of the physical. However, an aspect of the aura continues the journey; the memory and experience of our sacred human heart remains and is stored in the fourth level of the field, which is also the astral plain. The astral plain, or fourth level of the field, is governed by the heart chakra. At the time of death, the aura completely disconnects from the physical body; it is then, when spiritual animation ceases, that the body begins to decompose. However, the essence of our being continues the journey into unseen aspects of existence.

An illness in formation can be seen in the aura before it fully manifests in the body. We can be active in the creation of our own aura, the structure and the color, hence creating the well-being we desire.

The Chakra System

The chakra system is an integral part of the aura. It is a network of energetic vortices that regulate and optimize the vital flow of universal intelligence and life force energy throughout your body and your human energy field (your aura). Chakras are subtle energetic structures in the form of vortices that assist the physical body by helping to metabolize universal life force energy in order to inform, nurture, and heal the physical body. They are gateways of consciousness that can open and close at will, providing one knows how and is able to command the aura consciously.

Traditionally there are seven chakras that are said to make up the major chakra system. However, this is only true if we don't take into account the back aspect of a major chakra. Each chakra has a front and a back aspect. Each chakra has a very specific function, is alive, can change shapes, and opens and closes like a flower. The optimum state for a chakra is to be open and to spin clockwise (when looked at from the front).

Chakras are made of subtle lines of light and can be damaged or distorted by trauma, as they are not exempt from the rigors of life. Distortions or blockages may be caused by illness, accidents, stresses of modern life, difficult relationships, loss, or life-changing circumstances. A damaged or distorted chakra will limit or eliminate the vital flow of prana through its living structure. In some cases, the chakra itself has become obsolete so that the chakras above and below the nonfunctioning one will have to pick up the slack.

A distortion in a chakra will affect the health of the body, especially the part of the body that is governed by the distorted chakra. A chakra distortion may be noticed immediately by the energetically sensitive person. On the other hand, it may go unnoticed until there is physical fallout, weakness, or pain. The chakra structure allows for energetic respiration, or prana, to the governing area. Each chakra governs a specific area in the body, including mental, emotional, and spiritual aspects of your being.

For example, the front heart chakra, at the center of the chest, governs the physical heart, the lungs, the thymus, and the love energy in relationship to others and the world.

The back of the heart governs the thoracic spine and the medial aspect of the shoulder blades. The front aspect of the heart chakra tells us about the quality of love we are extending to others and to life in general. The back aspect tells us about our willingness to be loved by others. A telltale symptom of a closed heart chakra is continued criticism of others. Physical heart issues are always accompanied by a distortion of the heart chakra. Asthma and other lung issues are also related to heart chakra distortions. A closed chakra and back problems in the area of the shoulder blades indicate that one may carry too much of a burden without allowing loving support from others. A distorted or damaged chakra can be brought back to full functioning quite easily by restructuring. This can be done by a trained healer like myself. Or, over time, you can learn how to do this yourself.

The Seven Major Chakras: The Primary System

Here is a short overview of the seven major chakras, the primary system, which I will expand on in chapter 4.

First Chakra

Location: At the perineum and then opening toward the feet and into the ground

The first chakra is also called the grounding chakra. It is related to feeling safe in the physical body and to trust issues. This chakra governs the legs, feet, and knees; physical vitality; sexuality; and the ability to relax.

The first chakra's functioning is intimately connected with the second chakra. The highest manifestation of the first chakra is a full realization and connection with its counterpart, which is the seventh chakra. This is a marriage made in heaven and lived on earth. That is the promise of the fully realized aura and chakra system. It is universal intelligence, fully alive in the physical human form, in harmony and support of the individual and the greater good for all.

When closed or distorted, first chakra issues may include problems or weakness in the legs, knees, and feet; exhaustion and general lack of energy; inability to release past trauma; and living in a fear-based state.

Second Chakra, Front Aspect

Location: Center lower belly two to three inches above the pubic bone

A healthy functioning second chakra supports the emotional enjoyment of your own creation—the good feelings of you being you. The second chakra governs our emotional relationship with the self, as in self-love, creativity, and enjoyment of our sexuality. Physically, it governs the function of the reproductive system, large intestine, bladder, and urinary tract.

Second Chakra, Back Aspect

Location: Center of the sacrum

The back aspect up the second chakra regulates the quantity of life force, sexual energy, creative vitality, and the sacrum in the lower back.

Third Chakra, Front Aspect

Location: Solar plexus, upper stomach area

The front aspect of the third chakra governs the vital organs, the liver, gall bladder, stomach, pancreas, spleen, and small intestine and the quality of thoughts and belief systems. In positive reality, a healthy third chakra supports the natural authority of your unique being. Third chakra negative reality promotes personal power by way of competition and power over another.

Third Chakra, Back Aspect

Location: Mid back at the height of the kidneys

The third chakra in the back governs the mid to lower thoracic spine. This chakra supports your willingness to do what it takes to take care of yourself in all ways—to achieve physical, emotional, mental, and spiritual wellbeing.

Fourth Chakra, Front Aspect

Location: Center of the chest

The front aspect of the fourth chakra regulates the flow of love and joy through your body and your life. It governs the heart, lungs, thymus, and esophagus.

Fourth Chakra, Back Aspect

Location: Upper thoracic spine, between lower shoulder blades.

The back aspect of the heart chakra regulates the willingness to live in positive and loving reality with others and to receive the world as a loving place for who you are.

Fifth Chakra, Front Aspect

Location: Center of the throat

The fifth chakra governs the thyroid and the voice box. It is also involved in expression of authority through speech and voice. A healthy fifth chakra supports the intake and assimilation of all the good available to us at any time, like food or input from others. A conscious alignment with divine will in service of the greater good for all is most supportive of a fully functioning throat chakra.

Fifth Chakra, Back Aspect

Location: Cervical spine

A healthy functioning fifth chakra connects us to our life task or work in the world. A distorted fifth may result in a stiff or sore neck and issues with one's will. False pride is also signaled by a blocked fifth chakra in the back of the neck.

Sixth Chakra, Front Aspect

Location: Forehead between the brows

The sixth chakra in the front governs the frontal brain, the face, the eyes, and the pituitary. This chakra relates to divine love and connects us to our celestial reality and the noble mind, to love of nature, and to music and art. This center allows us to envision our future and to project it onto the screen of life.

Sixth Chakra, Back Aspect

Location: The back of the head

The sixth chakra in the back also governs the brain. It helps us execute our vision—to take it out of the conceptual realm and make it reality.

Seventh Chakra (Counterpart to the First Chakra)

Location: The crown of the head

The seventh chakra is the counterpart to the first chakra. It connects us to our creative genius of God and our God-given ability to create from nothing by being in touch with the sacred source of *all*. Here, we are connected to all that is, all that ever was, and all that ever will be; we are connected to that which we are an essential part of, opening to us the whole mystery of life and the universe. Here, information travels faster than the speed of light and is picked up by those who have their antennas out and are grounded in their purpose, mostly by individuals exercising their divine genius of God in service of evolving human life for all.

The seventh chakra governs the brain and higher aspirations of the noble mind. When in harmony with all aspects of your being, the seventh chakra is the crowning glory of you, as the unique individual you are—having claimed your divine genius of God.

The Secondary Chakra System

Location: At every joint in the body

Besides the primary chakra system, there is a secondary chakra system of smaller chakras, governing and supporting all of the joints and the organs in the body. Wherever there is a joint—for example, the shoulders, knees or hips—there is also a secondary chakra helping the joint to function properly. But even the smaller joints, such as the wrists, the fingers, and the toes have chakras.

In my practice, when someone presents a joint complaint, like knee or shoulder problems, I always check the secondary chakras first. Easily 98 percent of the time, the chakra governing the area of complaint will be distorted or will have gone void. The secondary chakra system can be restructured easily, just like the major chakra system. All chakra structures are made up of lines of light and alternately filled in with cloud-like, gaseous substance and integrate seamlessly into the rest of the aura.

The Hara, or Line of Intention

The hara, or line of intention, is the energetic anchor for your life purpose. A level deeper than the aura, the hara comes up from the earth; goes through the center of your bones, through the vertical power current, up and down the front of your spine. The hara is the tuning fork for our individual life purpose and fulfillment in life, and it holds within it the reason we have embodied this time around.

A "hara healing" or "hara line healing" is helpful and needed when you are searching for *your life purpose*, as your purpose is encoded in the hara. A hara healing is also beneficial when recovering from physical trauma or when seeking a life change.

A healthy hara is deeply supportive of physical health. When the hara is in good alignment, we tend to feel at home within ourselves and on target with our life purpose.

A damaged hara or a distortion in the hara line will have you feeling less like yourself and out of touch with your purpose. It often includes a lack of enjoyment in your life and body. The hara is one level deeper than the aura; it, therefore, defines the aura to a certain degree. The hara line goes through the center of your bones and in front of your spine through the vertical power current. When the hara is damaged or broken, we tend to have pain in the area where the hara is compromised, which can be marked by a weakness in functioning.

A hara line healing is usually done by a professional trained healer with years of experience. But this healing can also be initiated by oneself with advanced self-healing training. However, any kind of sustained, focused support on the hara with yoga, walking, or martial arts will gradually strengthen it.

Besides being deeply healing on a physical level, a hara alignment can bring about a supportive course correction to help fulfill one's ultimate life purpose. Your purpose makes itself known by the longing in your upper heart. That which you are longing for, your life purpose, is also longing for you! Beautiful isn't it?

The longing within the upper part of the hara, also called the soul seat, is your guiding light; it is the inner compass that guides you to your true north. It leads you, with pleasure in your own being, to that which gives you life and brings you true joy. That is how you know that you are on track with your purpose. *So in a way, the hara line is about the fun that you can have as the unique individual that you are.* Less fun and even suffering occurs if you are too far off track.

Distortions of the hara and the field can be the result of accidents or illness, as well as someone else's agenda. An example is when parents raise their children with their own expectations and aspirations, rather then guiding each child to his or her own unique expression of purpose and essence.

The Four Points to the Hara

The hara has five unique points:

1) The first point is actually outside your body in the earth. It is your body's personal connection with the earth at the center of the earth. In a way, this energetic connection symbolizes our interconnectedness with the greater whole. This point is ultimately grounding and supports you in your life's purpose. It is your anchor. Physical practice helps it to align; yoga, martial arts, walking, and hiking are practices that are most supportive of a healthy hara.

2) The dan tien point in the center of the lower belly is at the height of the hip bone and to the front of the sacrum. It is a liquid ball of fire in your free belly. It is the active intention in alignment with what you are longing for. This is the sacred fire in your belly for what cannot be denied! This fire in your lower belly burns to fulfill the longing of

your inner heart's dream; it yearns to make this dream real in the physical world, in the here and now.

3) The third point of the hara is the longing, or the soul seat. It is located in the center chest and upper heart. This is where we tend to place our hands when we are talking about something that really matters to us. This place, the soul seat, is alive with our longing or inner heart's dream. When it is shrouded, we do not know what we really want and tend to follow other people's protocol. Generally, the state of the heart chakra plays an important role in being able to access and feel into one's longing. If the heart chakra has been diminished, closed, or distorted for a while, even the notion of *longing* may feel outlandish and out of touch with one's experience of a daily dull humdrum "reality."

4) The fourth point of the hara is your personal connection to source, or God. It is located about a foot to a foot and half above your head. Like the first point of the hara it also located outside of your body, connecting to the spiritual dimension and forming your personal connection to God. When this place is activated with ultimate alignment, you are present to your longing, aligned, and grounded in your intention. Then all things tend to fall into place, helping you to make your longing and inner heart's dream come true. Also, your own God-given genius is activated, giving you brilliant insights, support, and guidance in the right direction.

The hara goes through the center of your bones and helps them heal when broken. Meditation, martial arts, hiking, dance, and yoga are wonderful means to build, support, and strengthen your hara. Intentional brisk walking with awareness on all four hara points is also excellent preparation for a hara healing.

The hara is synonymous with purpose. Your hara serves to support your purpose in physical reality all the way down into your body, literally down to your bones. When you are in your hara, you have purpose in your bones and are able to access the deep inner wisdom of your being through the ages naturally, as it relates to your purpose. When you are in your hara, it is easy to harness and harvest positive past life experience in service of your purpose. In other words, all that you have been and have mastered in other lives can come forward to help you manifest your dream.

Your Core Star

Your core star, at the center of your being, is the ever-present light of your creative God presence. Your core star radiates your creative God spark from the center of your being. It is the sum total of your pure light energy, which shines with the signature of your unique individuality. It is the light of your essence—that which you have been for time eternity and which you add to with each life.

Your core star is the *essence of your being*. When out of touch with this essence, we tend to look for too much outer validation and might anchor to a masked personality existence. In other words, we might accumulate possessions, personality traits, and even people, which we identify with in an attempt to fill that inner void. Addiction is a most severe manifestation of being out of touch with one's essence.

When in touch with your essence, you know who you are because you feel and enjoy the light of your being. Others can see and feel it too. It is easy to see and feel the true light of another. It is just as easy to spot someone trying too hard. The person feels deep inside that something is amiss and can't quite connect with him or herself. This disconnection is the result of a shrouding or a wounding. These wounds can go back lifetimes and are called soul traumas. Soul traumas create a greater shrouding and can be addressed with past-life healing. Core star healing is usually done in combination with hara healing.

Your unique consciousness, combined with the universal intelligence of life, is a winning combination that will help you heal and thrive in all areas of your life. By joining forces with universal intelligence, you are becoming a conscious cocreator. Think of yourself as a conscious cocreator with life itself. Imagine the possibilities. But you would have to consciously choose to be a cocreator with the divine.

I am inviting you, from here on out, to consider yourself a spiritual being inhabiting a human body. Invite more of your spirit body—the light of your being. Imagine your spirit or light body merging into your physical body by request, like hands into gloves and feet into socks.

Elevate and illuminate your physical existence with the eternal spark of life that is your core star. Take charge of your existence by choosing to be alive. Choosing to be here is the first step—choosing to be alive and conscious in the physical body as who and what you are. You are life itself. You are the magic of life and unique at that. You already have a unique blueprint inside of you, a blueprint that has been a part of you from the time you were born. Make it your mission to activate your God-given blueprint to fulfill your purpose, the reason you have taken a physical body this time around.

You are not flying blind. You already have an inner compass guiding you at all times in the direction of your purpose. That compass is called your heart flame, your inner heart's dream, or your longing. Your inner heart's dream is the source code encrypted in your hara. Your IHD will guide you through your longing toward that which gives you joy, keeps you interested, and gives you life. When your life choices resonate with your hara, you know you are on track. You are likely to feel the joy of your uniqueness, as you will be contributing to others and living from the essence of your being. It all fits, and life flows harmoniously, bringing you all that you need.

Feel inside of you, into the empty space—the space that is seeking fulfillment. Connect to your heart flame, your inner heart's dream. What wants to come alive, to be experienced by you? What will bring you joy? Is there a special gift that wants to be cultivated and given to the world? Is there a latent talent to be nurtured and refined to mastery? What pulls you in and won't let you go?

It may take a little courage to fully feel your IHD and not succumb to the voices of negative reality. The all-too-familiar discouraging comments that won't even let you out of the starting gate may come over you with a vengeance, bringing up old wounds and traumas. They'll list all kinds of reasons you won't succeed or tell you why it is not possible or convenient right now to fulfill your inner heart's dream. Allow them to be there and don't fight them. These are old voices, habits, and loops of thinking (and being) that don't serve you anymore. Be calm and witness negative self-talk without reaction. Just notice. What are you telling yourself? You might even want to write down your thoughts to get it all out. Then decide who and what you want to be. Reframe your thoughts so that your thinking supports your endeavor.

Spiritual reality is wonderful to turn to for support and inspiration, but we have to do all that we can in the physical reality to pull our own weight. We must put the stake into the ground to hold up our end of the deal. We have to build a solid foundation with our physical practice that will aid us in fully receiving and utilizing all the good available to us.

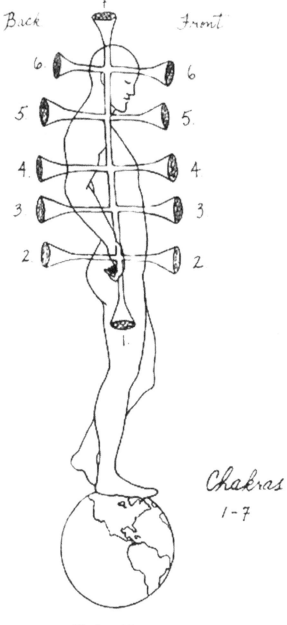

Back   Front

7

6.   6

5.   5.

4.   4.

3   3

2.   2

1.

Chakras
1-7

Chakra King

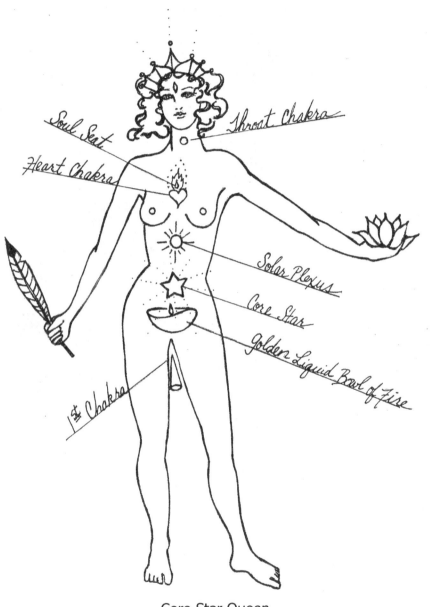

Soul Seat

Throat Chakra

Heart Chakra

Solar Plexus

Core Star

Golden Liquid Bowl of Fire

1st Chakra

Core Star Queen

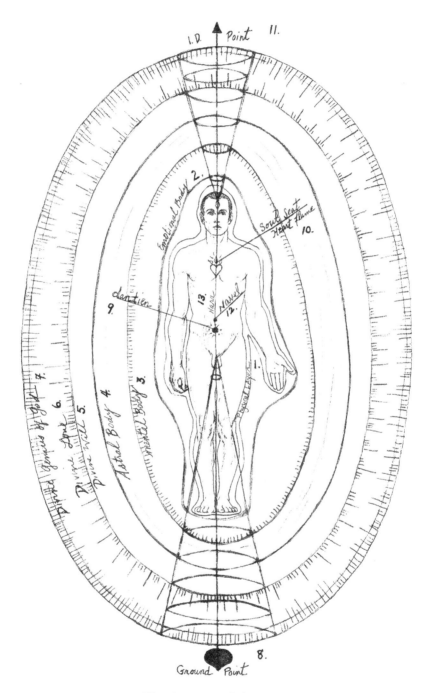

The Layers of the Field

Aura
7 Layers of the Field
Hara Line

1. Physical
2. Emotional
3. Mental
4. Astral
5. Divine Will
6. Divine Love
7. Divine Genius of God
8. Ground Point Earth
9. dan tien
10. Soul Seat Heart Flame
11. I. D. Point
12. Navel
13. Hara

Chapter 3

YOUR FIRST CHAKRA: THE FOUNDATION OF YOUR GOOD HEALTH AND PHYSICAL VITALITY

The ultimate promise and opportunity of the first chakra is the celebration of spirit in the flesh.

—Karin Inana

A healthy first chakra provides the foundation for a fully functioning field and a vital physical experience. Understanding the functioning of the first chakra is so important that I have devoted a whole chapter to it. I will refer back to the first chakra throughout this book to underline its importance to the vitality of the aura as a whole.

Let's continue by checking in with your physical reality, the physical reality of your body and your first chakra. Is the state of your physical body in alignment with your purpose? Does your body feel and function the way you want it to? Would you like to feel better in some way? Are you hurting and ill? Are fear and anxiety running rampant in your life and ruining your joy? Most of us desire for our body and our health to be better. A healthy first chakra assists us in this task, naturally.

The following is a simple statement of truth that supports the first chakra when you say it out loud. Try it now and see how you feel when you say it:

I am life! We are, you are, I am—life itself!

Contemplate this statement for a moment and say out loud:

I am life. I am life itself! Conscious, ever-evolving life, I am that!

The ultimate promise and opportunity of the first chakra is the celebration of spirit in the flesh. It is the ability for us to fully enjoy being fully alive, in our bodies, on earth with all this life has to offer. It enables our enjoyment of good food and fresh water; helps us touch, feel, sense and delight in physical experiences; supports healthy, loving relationships; and allows us to enjoy sex, sports, and rock and roll. The first chakra helps us enjoy our aliveness in positive relationship with life itself by governing the sensations of the physical body.

The highest manifestation of the first chakra is a full realization of the connection with its counterpart, the seventh chakra. This is a marriage made in heaven and lived on earth. It is the completion of the avatar body, the promise of the fully realized aura and chakra system. Finally, we come alive as universal intelligence in physical human form, in harmony and support of the individual, and for the greater good of all.

The first chakra helps to ground us in physical reality, as it provides the energetic link between the earth and the human body, facilitating a symbiotic exchange and a flow of energy that is mutually supportive. The first chakra enlivens our experience with heightened sensation, taste, and smell. When it is fully functioning, we tend to feel calm and trust in our relationship with life.

The first chakra governs our legs and spine with stabilizing earth energy. It also supports our nervous system, kidneys, and adrenal function. With a healthy first chakra, we are in tune with our bodies. We know when and what to eat or drink, when to rest, and what kind of exercise will suit us best. A fully functioning first chakra supports a positive relationship with our human body and the earth. Trusting ourselves, we make the right choices and enjoy life's fecundity.

A distorted first chakra will compromise, diminish, and dull your ability to sense and feel. You may feel disconnected from your body without knowing why and exhausted but unable to rest deeply. Anxiety, along with a futile feeling of spinning your wheels, undermines the joy of life as stress accumulates in your nervous system. When you are unable to release the mounting stress through your legs back into the ground, the symbiotic relationship between your body and the earth is blocked. As nurturing earth energies are eluding you, you begin to feel separate and disconnected from nature and life as a whole.

This disconnection leads one further astray. Now, in order to solve the physical energy crisis, you may reach unconsciously and unfortunately for sugar; drink; or, worse, drugs. Doing so deepens the divide and furthers the cycle of erosion; the ground literally slips away from underneath your feet, leaving you feeling alienated and unsupported by life.

How does a chakra get distorted or blocked? The parenting we receive can have a lot to do with the state of our first chakra. If you were nurtured and brought up in a safe environment without physical or emotional trauma, you have a fairly good chance of having a healthy functioning first chakra. Physical trauma, like giving birth, accidents, or continued abuse, are likely to derail the positive alignment of the first chakra and distort the physical experience. I have worked with quite a few new mothers who had a difficult time recovering their energy after giving birth, even two years after childbirth. As the birth canal goes right through the first chakra, at the perineum, the lines of light that make up the first chakra can get torn and distorted when bringing the baby into this world naturally. When this is not addressed, it can add stress to the mother down the road, as a distorted first chakra will prevent the body from releasing trauma and stress back into the earth, stress than builds up in the mother's body, causing overwhelm and more distortion in the aura.

If fear was the main motivator in your upbringing, chances

are, you don't know what it feels like to have a supporting first chakra experience. In other words, you would not feel safe in your body or in the world. For example, an overly authoritarian military parent threatening dire consequences at every turn would surely induce a constant feeling of fear in a child. Sustained fear will leave the child with a pervasive low-grade anxiety, pestering him or her at all times. Talking about it and understanding "why" will help only so much. Growing up in a war-torn country causes similar distortions in the first chakra (and of course other chakras as well), causing a perpetual sense of fear and anxiety. Eventually, the culprit called fear has to be released from the nervous system, as well as from the emotional and mental aspects of the field. It is only then—when the fear has left and the nervous system is neutral once again—that one can feel oneself as who one is (in his or her own essence). A newly restructured first chakra will present a whole new perspective and a calmer reality, often a reality that was previously beyond reach.

If a longstanding illness prompts you to seek help with recovery, a restructuring and recalibration of the first chakra can work wonders for you, helping to revitalize your body and to speed up the healing process.

I have had clients on my table marveling with wonder during a first chakra healing. Thirty minutes into the session, their legs come alive with a tingling sensation that is followed by a deep relaxation. For many of my clients, this is the first time in years or decades that they have been able to enjoy a truly calm state of being. "I can feel myself" is a common expression uttered by clients when the first chakra comes alive during a healing session. I cannot stress enough the importance of a healthy functioning first chakra. In a series of healing sessions, it is almost always the starting point. The dramatic change from beginning to end of this session is fun for me to witness and confirms the effectiveness of this work.

First chakra restructuring is helpful when dealing with sexual trauma or dysfunction or if you are seeking to release physical trauma of any kind, from accidents, abuse, or illness. Issues with the feet, knees, and legs are helped along in the healing process. In many cases, working with the first chakra is the only thing that will bring about lasting relief.

As a child in Germany, I was debilitated by an omnipresent sense of fear. Fear surrounded me. It was everywhere. It was in the bodies of those who had live through the Second World War, and the ground was soaked with it, even decades after my birth. It was not a good situation for a sensitive, empathic child like me.

I had my whole field restructured and recalibrated numerous times, especially my first and second chakras. My mother was a little girl when the bombs were falling, and I inherited her fear in the womb while she was pregnant with me. Plus, children learn through harmonic induction from their parents, mostly from their mothers. I was born into a state of pervasive fear, so threatening that there was no sense of physical safety to be found—not after the war, not in my family, and not in Germany for me. The ground itself was vibrating with leftover fear, guilt, and helplessness. And I absorbed it all, believing that it was within me.

I don't remember ever feeling safe when I was a child, except when I was playing in nature. Being around other humans made me timid and scared. I did not know why I felt so strange when being around others. I was uncomfortable in my own skin most of the time, except when I was alone.

One day, before I was admitted to my first grade school, my mother decided that it would be a good idea to teach me how to read. Her attempt, initially based in good intentions, proved itself to be detrimental and ultimately undermined my ability to learn, making my future as a student quite difficult.

I remember feeling small. Her ominous presence bent over me from behind my chair; a sharp finger pointed and tapped the page at the line she wanted me to focus on. She screamed into my ear, "Read!" My mother's shrill high-pitched voice pierced my ears, shattered my ability to focus, and dismantled my confidence as my thoughts disbursed in all directions like a scared flock of birds at a loud noise. In that moment, I felt like hellfire had descended on me, singeing the tender filigree of my still forming nervous system.

The effects of that incident reached far into my future—all the way into the here and now. In the past, the trauma of that event has limited me, as learning under pressure was a minefield. Most times I was asked to perform "on the spot," I got brain freeze. When this hellfire descended on me, part of my consciousness left my body. I remember just floating up and out into the silence above my body. I did not do anything to initiate this, but I felt safer, removed from the chaos of this verbal assault to be sure.

Over time, with repetition of similar assaults, my first chakra stopped functioning and became obsolete. As a result when I floated up and out of my body, I was not able to hear what others were saying, as I was so disconnected, I would only see their mouths moving but was not able to comprehend the meaning of the words spoken. I learned later on that leaving one's body is a common defense mechanism that is triggered when children or adults are being abused or experiencing extreme trauma. But because of the disconnection and because I was struggling to hear, secretly, I feared that I had some kind of brain damage.

It took me years to let it all go and yet a few more to heal myself into an experience of wholeness. Today, for the most part, I enjoy a wonderful peace and calm in my body and my life. I know that none of what I experienced had anything to do with who I am, other than being a sensitive being. I have forgiven all, including my late mother and father. And I am grateful for the knowledge my journey has offered up, as it has become most useful in my healing practice.

Restructuring and working with your first chakra will help release the fear and increase feelings of safety in your own body and in the world. Reestablishing trust and calm as a physically grounding experience will help to heal foot, knee, and hip issues. Increasing sensations in your physical body, restructuring your first chakra will assist in the healing and the release of sexual trauma and can improve sexual function when combined with other practices.

Any kind of healing is greatly assisted with a healthy newly recalibrated first chakra. One of my teachers, Barbara Ann Brennan, writes in her book, *Hands of Light*, that most diseases can be traced back to a malfunctioning first chakra.

Paying attention to your first chakra will help get your balancing system back on line. Restructuring the first chakra helps you to connect to the feelings and the sensations of the body. Hence, you have a way of tracking the messages your body is signaling.

Before restructuring a first chakra, the first thing I ask a client to do is to pay attention to his or her feet. There tends to be a distinct change in feeling the feet, from the inside out all the way into one's toes after a first chakra restructuring. It is like having your feet close to a campfire; they feel warm, cozy, and alive. Often, clients will say that they have not felt their feet in this way for some time or ever.

The sense of taste also seems to improve, sometimes dramatically. One client returned after a first chakra restructuring to tell me about a fantastic strawberry taste extravaganza. He told me it was like eating the berries for the very first time.

Sex is also known to get better. I have had some glowing reports come back to me, satisfied smiles included! And we all know how sweet rest can be after a good lovemaking session.

When our first chakra is healthy, we feel in tune with our bodies and enjoy the physical experiences of life. Resting comes more easily with a healthy first chakra.

Exercise to Begin Clearing Your First Chakra

- The statement is, "I am life. I am life itself."
- Take about ten minutes for this practice.
- Sit with a straight spine with your feet on the ground.
- Observe, relax, and feel into the ebb and flow of your breath.
- Direct your inner gaze (with your eyes closed) to your perineum, where the narrow tip of your first chakra comes into the vertical power current. The wide part of the chakra opens to the feet and the ground beneath you.
- What do you feel here (from the pubic bone down to the earth)?
- What do your legs and feet feel like? Are your legs alive with energy? Can you feel your toes?
- Keeping your inner gaze on your perineum and your breath steady, relax into the area of your first chakra.
- Do you see a color? Do you feel a movement of energy? Do you feel calm or agitated?
- If you have a question about your first chakra, ask it out loud. You may get an answer immediately or in the following hours. The question may be, "What does my first chakra need most at this time?"
- End your session by saying, "I am life, I am life itself," and then, "Thank you," out loud.

The ideal color of the first chakra is a bright red. It can also be dark red or muddy brown when distorted. When you are starting out, you may not feel or see much. Don't be discouraged, even if you don't get anything at first; the practice itself will improve your first chakra health for the better, and you'll get more detailed information about your first chakra as you continue to practice.

You carry Mother Earth within you. She is not outside of you. Mother Earth is not just your environment. In that insight of inter-being, it is possible to have real communication with the Earth, which is the highest form of prayer.

—Thich Nhat Hanh

Healing Skill: Walking as a Healing Practice

There is nothing better than a good, long, and brisk walk to assist your first chakra in functioning. Not to mention all the other health benefits to your body, like increased circulation, oxygenation, improved brain function, and better joint mobility. There is no better way to activate your first chakra for your daily healing practice than with a good walk on mother earth.

The earth is a living being in partnership with all other living beings. This partnership can be especially supportive in terms of energy healing. Have you ever noticed how relaxing and refreshing a walk can be? Has a walk ever made you feel more alive, awake, and happy or inspired you? My answer to those questions is yes, yes, and yes! Walking to me is magical, rejuvenating, and healing. I love to walk, especially uphill. I love to walk hills and mountains. I love the way it gets me breathing and out of my head and into my legs. I enjoy the feeling of the earth underneath my feet and the way nature's beauty opens my heart, every time. I don't think I have ever regretted going on a walk. But I am likely to lament a missed opportunity to connect with myself and mother earth on a particularly beautiful day because an important, or not so important call, got the better of me.

Walking is one of those simple and richly rewarding joys. It makes you feel good. It's just so good for your health and can be healing in and of itself. It cost nearly nothing, except for a good pair of walking shoes and the proper weather attire. Really, most of us have a pair of shoes that are comfortable enough to take a walk in. And if you are lucky enough to live near a beach, well then, you don't need shoes at all. If you happen to live in a city or small town, a walk in your neighborhood might be just as much fun. You might enjoy looking at houses, front lawns, and gardens. Beautiful architecture and people watching can make a walk in the city fun and interesting.

The health benefits of walking are obvious. It aids circulation, inspires breathing, speeds up the metabolism, and wakes up the brain. The benefits are hailed and talked about in detail by countless health professionals. Julia Cameron, author of *The Artist's Way,* writes in *Walking in This World* at length about walking as a creatively nurturing, inspirational, and spiritual practice. It all works for me. Walking has been a lifelong practice of mine, helping me to connect to my innermost feelings and leave negative thinking on the trail. It connects me to myself and helps me receive guidance, not to mention the wonders it does for my first chakra and hara. The first chakra is our grounding chakra. It governs the legs, the knees, and the feet, as well as the nervous system and the spinal column. A closed first chakra disconnects us from the feelings and sensations of our physical body. We tend to be more mental and prone to worry when our grounding is missing. And worse, one might live in a perpetual state of fear. The legs may be affected, feeling weak, uncoordinated, and restless at the same time. One might be tired but restless when going to bed and unable to get quality sleep because of a distortion in the grounding chakra. The first chakra connects us to the earth and helps us release stress from the body and into the ground. Nurturing earth energy, by way of walking, can help you rest, relax, and sleep better at night.

Personally, I always wonder what is behind the restless leg syndrome TV advertisement. Are the legs restless because they want more movement, or is it a true syndrome? And then, what is a true syndrome? When "restless legs" happen to me, it is a sure sign I need to take myself for a good walk. Even when my mind tells me I am too tired, afterward I am always happy I went.

Tips on Walking as a Healing Practice

Before heading out the door, make sure you are comfortable with your clothing and shoes. For longer walks, you might want to take some water with you. Consider a sun visor if you go out on a sunny day or a flashlight for your night walks. Intention transforms your walk into a spiritual practice, or a prayer. What is the focus of your walk going to be about? How far or for how long are you committing to walk? How much time do you have? Are you walking for inspiration and energy, or do you want to let go of a negative situation and transform it into a positive? If you have a question, walk with that question. Ask for assistance of the unseen world that walks with you and by your side.

Whether you go fast or slow, notice the movement of your body and how it feels. Get a steady momentum going and stay with it. Adjust your position, align your spine, and reach up out of your crown while enjoying the support of the earth underneath your feet. Is one part of your body working harder than another? Do you lean forward while looking at the ground? Or do you feel rigid and tightly held back? How are you relating to your surroundings and other people? Are you open or closed off?

You can change the experience of your walk by adjusting your attitude and body alignment. When you are satisfied with your positioning, you can focus on enjoyment or inner questions. The living light aspects of God will respond to your requests of guidance, and your unseen friends are sure to walk with you to inspire your heartfelt quest.

Healing Skill: Statement for a Healing Walk

Here is your statement to initiate your healing walk to wake up your first chakra:

It is my choice and intention to move, to wake up, and to enliven my body. I declare this walk to be a healing event to wake up my first chakra. And that is my choice!

You can expand upon that command as you wish, and you may want to invite members of your MDST to walk with you for guidance on a specific matter.

Healing Skill: Resting (Also see chapter 5, "The Art of Resting and Receiving.")

Resting when healing is like water to fish, an absolutely essential aspect.

After your walk, take ten to fifteen minutes to rest on your back and integrate and absorb your experience. Give your body the space and permission to receive all the good you have generated. Lie on your back, perhaps with a pillow under your knees and a support for your neck. Make sure you are absolutely comfortable, cover your eyes, and let go.

With the first few breaths, let go of all your thoughts; breathe them out and come into this moment. Feel the ebb and flow of your breath in your chest. Then become present to your limbs, hands, and feet. Let them rest on the bed or floor. Feel the support underneath you and receive it fully. Then become present to the skin of your face and how your breath flows in through your nose and mouth, down into your lungs, to the heart. Now take the path of your newly oxygenated blood flowing through and nurturing your brain organs and tissues.

Connect with your heartbeat and observe your breath. There is nothing you have to do for the moment other than feel life pulsing in your chest and breathing you. Let life breathe you! Indeed, we don't have to think about beating our own heart or taking our next breath; the intelligence of life itself that is innate in our own body will do this for us. Relax into your breath, knowing that you are connected to the creative intelligence of life itself and observe your breath, rather than directing it. This alone can be a revelation in healing. Try it; it can change your life.

Resting is the counterpart to movement and meditation. They go hand in hand. Resting compliments and completes the healing sequence of your walk or meditation. If you have thirty or forty-five minutes, even better, as that is enough time to request and command a healing for yourself.

Longing from the Distant Past: Past-Life Trauma and First Chakra Health

Three weeks into my writing project, just as I got to writing about the first chakra, I promptly stubbed the fourth toe of my right foot on the foot of my bed while attempting to make my bed. There was this awful little crunch and then—ouch! I looked down at my foot and found my forth toe a little loose and disconnected. Afraid that I had broken it, I checked it out in detail and determined that only tendons and perhaps a smaller ligament had been affected. There was no sharp pain, and I was able to walk on it. I was grateful it was not broken. But it slowed me down significantly and took a little bit longer than expected to heal. Yoga and hiking were out of the question for at least a few days. After four days of self-care and healing, I resumed hiking but at a much slower pace and covering less distance too. After two weeks, the healing of my toe seemed to have come to a standstill. My toe was particularly sore at night and in the early morning when I got up. I sensed a past life overlay at work, partly because of the pain spreading out and moving around in my foot. Also telling was the fact that the healing did not seem to be progressing.

I called a dear friend of mine who is a deeply sensitive being and a healer in his own right. Gunther came to help. As I related to him my suspicion of a past life overlay working my foot, we both saw, spontaneously and at the same time, a wagon wheel crushing all of the toes on my right foot, save the big toe. The carriage was halted. I was a young girl about to enter when the horse, spooked by something, stepped forward, moving the carriage just enough for the wagon wheel to roll over of my right foot. The toes were crushed at the level of the third metatarsals, breaking most of the fine bones in the front of my right foot. As

Gunther gently massaged my foot, helping to repair the lines of light that had been broken while stubbing the toe, more of the past life made itself known.

I had been a girl, perhaps ten or eleven, with my whole life ahead of me when this incident occurred in the distant past. Because this was largely before modern medicine, not much could be done to help the foot heal correctly. In time, it became clear that this event had changed the course of my life. The foot healed eventually but in an unfortunate way. Due to the fact that the body of the young girl/my body was still growing at the time of the accident, the bones never healed with proper alignment, and the crippled foot became a source of never-ending pain and anguish. Over time, my walk changed into an awkward, lopsided gait. Walking on the flattened arch of my mangled right foot threw my whole body out of balance, making me look unappealing to myself and possible suitors.

This seemingly small incident had changed the course of the girl's life. The reason this incident surfaced now was *the unfulfilled longing this story holds*. I could feel it clearly, the dreams of that young life that had been crushed as the bones of the foot had been broken. Both my friend and I witnessed this event with compassion and understanding, acknowledging a life and longing unfulfilled. My foot in present time advanced to heal immediately.

How Longing from Past Lives Can Relate to the First Chakra Health

Interestingly enough, another piece of the puzzle relating to longing and the first chakra also surfaced right around the time I started writing *Heart Flame Healing*. The foods we eat are intimately related to the health of the first chakra, as the first chakra is all about the quality of our physical experience.

Eight months prior, I suddenly became intolerant to sugar. Seemingly overnight I broke out in a form of itchy, blistering dermatitis that made mincemeat out of my right hand and threatened to take over my whole body. Within a day, a yearlong annoyance of small itchy blisters on my right middle finger escalated into a full-blown crisis. My right hand looked awful and itched relentlessly; it was swollen and hurting. The day it came front and center, I cried in despair on my way to and from my office going home. I called my friend and discussed the matter. I had researched dermatitis, and the known treatment options were creams and steroid shots. However, guidance told me repeatedly not to go the medical route.

When I got home that evening, I prayed for help and additional specific information. That night I had visions of my guides taking me down a food buffet. We walked down long aisles of various foods cooking in pots and boiling over. I was not sure why they were showing this to me, as my diet had been relatively healthy for most of my life. However, the next morning, I woke up knowing that I had to pendulum all of my foods before consuming anything to make sure what I was about to eat agreed with me.

Surprise, I found I was left with hardly anything but greens, vegetables, leafy greens, legumes, and a few nuts. Any form of sugar checked out as negative for me, as did grain products like bread and pasta. I was also advised via the pendulum to stay away from meat, fruit, wine, and cheese for the moment. I heeded the advice without hesitation and got better, for the most, part within a week.

To this day, my diet remains largely restricted. I consume no sugar, no grain or bread, and hardly any fruits, except some organic berries as a treat now and then. On occasion, I can enjoy trout, but I eat no other fish or meat. Chocolate and wine have been eliminated. I don't really have a problem with my new diet. For the most part, following it is easy for me.

But one day, during the height of summer, the cherries looked so tasty. While shopping for groceries, I was unable to resist them. I picked up a pound and gave them a try. They were so good, and I loved them so much that I ate the whole pound in one sitting. So far so good—my hands were holding up.

The next time I went to the store, I picked up some more of

those yummy big red cherries, two pounds this time. I ate them all, a pound for lunch and a pound for dinner. I was starved for fruit. I had been without the natural sweet of fruits for months now and had always loved it so much. Unable to stop myself, the next time I went to the store, I bought more cherries. I looked for the biggest sweetest ones but did myself no favors by eating the sixth pound.

The next morning, I woke up with my right hand, the middle finger in particular, itching, blistering, and swelling up. The sugar from the cherries had accumulated in my system, feeding the condition and making it bloom again. Dismayed, I gave the rest of the cherries away for my neighbor's kids to enjoy.

My midsummer cherry extravaganza set off a whole new cycle of dermatitis again. This time, I knew what to do and pulled back immediately. Still, it took a while for the reaction to clear out of my finger and hand. I felt several layers at work: Due to my increased vibrational frequency because of the healing work I do, I had become intolerant to sugar, grain, flower, meat, and wine. But beyond the physical layer, I sensed that typical prickly, vibrational telltale accompanying a past-life overlay.

I am no stranger to past-life occurrences underlying physical issues. I had gone there before to explore this skin issue and came up with a lifetime of a leper, an aversion to cotton picking, and a life of spinning wool—all of which made sense to me given what I was dealing with.

One morning after my cherry orgy, my right middle finger was swollen and hurting again, so much so that I was not able to bend it at the first joint. Guided to do some more past-life exploration and healing, I held my finger and went into the forth layer of the field, the astral layer, the one holding past lives. What unraveled before my inner eyes and mind were lifetimes of ordinary drudgery and human hardship I had endured through the ages. Again I saw the lives of cotton picking, planting, spinning wool, and weaving. In one life, I watched myself digging up the crusty earth with my bare hands and, while doing so, detaching the nail of my right middle finger. A small rock had caught underneath the nail and torn it off, resulting in a pulsing, puss-filled infection that invaded the nail bed—and would not heal. Next, I witnessed the amputation of the right middle finger at the second joint, by way of it being hacked off. Ouch! By staying with the images and feelings, I discovered what this dermatitis was all about. These were not violent traumas I was witnessing; this was ordinary life. I was seeing the hard monotony of life before the industrial revolution, the long hours of doing one task over and over for a whole life long.

In one past life image, I held a leather pouch in my hand. I wondered what was in it. It felt like a treasure to me. Was it money? I asked myself as I was watching this on my inner mind's screen. Then I saw the seeds. I held them in my hands. These precious seeds were going to be my new fortune. I saw myself planting and nurturing them into stalks of something big. And then they disappeared. Then anger rose in my face—so much anger I could feel the emotional heat rising to the surface of my face in present time.

Believing all was lost, I was angry with God, the weather, or others. It mattered not, I had lost the dream of my new fortune and a better life. It dawned on me then that this was why all these lifetimes rose in my consciousness now. It was for the unfulfilled longing of the past that parts of my being still called out to be known. These were the sacred echoes of that longing sounding in my heart of hearts. I saw and felt all the hardship gone before—the hours, days, and years. I saw lifetimes of monotony endured with patience but filled with distant dreams of freedom and a better life—dreams that were now fulfilled. Gifts of wisdom returned on a wave of gratitude, and I knew with certainty that true healing is holographic and retroactive indeed.

Even with my toe in distress and my hands bearing reminders, sacred tattoos of lifetimes gone by, I had never felt happier or more fulfilled. I said to all of my parts that had endured, suffered, and dreamed, "You have made it; you are part of the whole. Thank you for your gift."

Chapter 4

A DEEPER LOOK INTO THE AURA: THE SECOND TO SEVENTH CHAKRAS

The aura is our multidimensional support system,
without which we would have no life.

—Karin Inana

Second Chakra

The promise of a healthy functioning second chakra front and back is self-love and the enjoyment of one's own creation, fueled by plenty of positive life-force energy. Hallmarks are contentment when resting and being energized while actively pursuing one's creation. The front aspect of the second chakra lends emotional quality to the experience, while the back aspect cheers on with quantity of sexual, creative life-force energy, supplying mojo for the task.

In women, the front aspect of the second chakra rules over procreation with a quality of receptivity. And in males, the back aspect rules physical creation with quantity of vital sexual life-force energy, ensuring success by providing more.

Distortions in the second chakra are emotionally painful or

numbing, depending on the severity of the trauma precluding the distortion. Women with small children in particular suffer more from distortions of the second chakra. Mothers, out of necessity, closely connect to their children physically and emotionally, mostly forgetting about themselves, as time for self-care is limited while caring for a small child, even more so with multiple children.

We tend to lose our own inner emotional compass by giving endlessly. Often forgetting to include ourselves, we nurture others and give until there is no more, leaving us holding an empty cup. Emotionally, this can be a very unhappy situation. It can leave us numb or frozen; at first, one might not notice the joy of one's own being slipping away. A lackluster cloud of dullness accumulates around the heart, and soon it takes all of our energy to get out of bed in the morning. And for what? In my practice, I have noticed that depression is a common diagnosis for women with severe second chakra distortions, especially if it is in combination with a lack of grounding.

Then, we are spinning like busybodies on a hamster wheel until some kind of crisis, either physical or emotional, stops us in our tracks. Hopefully, we go looking for help.

Sexual trauma present and past underlies most severe second chakra distortions, providing the emotional wallpaper with a pervasive sense of shame and guilt. But in addition, a cold or abusive parent can leave a lasting negative imprint in the emotional body, stealing the creative joy of life until it is reclaimed through extensive healing.

Physically, the front of the second chakra governs the reproductive system, the large intestine, the bladder, and the urinary tact. The back aspect of the second chakra rules over the sacrum and lumbar spine. Lower back pain is the most common result of this distortion.

The second chakra represents our emotional relationship with ourselves; when it is fully functioning, we feel like ourselves and enjoy the good feelings of being ourselves. Self-love is a natural experience of the healthy emotional life. *The true statement of the second chakra is, "I feel myself as I am. There is no need to change anything."* Knowing that it is safe to feel all that life presents to us, we don't have to defend against anything. Anger, sadness, joy, disappointment, jealousy, or envy can pass through without judgment because we know we can return to our natural state of being in harmony with ourselves. Emotions are then what they are supposed to be, providing the full palate of color to life. Emotions are messages of the heart. They provide information about how to navigate our relationships, including our relationship with the self. And they help us evolve to a higher ground of consciousness and a greater enjoyment of our being.

To explain the effect of a second chakra restructuring to my clients, I like to say, "Get ready to feel the yumminess of your being." For many individuals, this is a missing experience. But they do connect to the term *yummy* immediately, knowing exactly what they might have been missing.

For those of you who are reading this and are not able to book a second chakra restructuring, the following is a meditation and visualization, which if done in regular intervals, will strengthen your second chakra and help clear your emotional body.

The Golden Liquid Bowl of Fire

Visualize your pelvic bowl as an actual energetic bowl—a container filled with a life-giving liquid fire. See the red of the first chakra; here are the embers out of which the warm orange flames of the second chakra rise. These beautiful, vital orange flames are warm rather than hot and deeply nourishing. At the top licks the yellow flame of the healthy mind, bringing understanding to the emotions that are being processed. This is followed by the green of the heart chakra. And finally, the violet flame of divine love consumes and purifies the rest, leaving only pure creative energy for greater enjoyment of your being.

- As you begin this exercise, say out loud to yourself, "I feel myself as who and what I am only. There is no need to change anything." By doing so, you give yourself permission to feel all there is to feel without judgment. There is nothing to do about it; just observe and allow.

- Then move to visualize your golden liquid fire bowl. Notice the shape and size of it. See the red hue that makes up the flame rising from the first chakra and then see it turning to a warm nurturing orange.
- Feel the warmth rising from the flames warming your pelvis. Allow yourself to be with whatever comes up. Be your own witness and observe while continuing to breathe gently into your pelvis.
- Sit in your golden liquid bowl of fire for at least five minutes a day, and your emotional life will change for the better. Enjoy the warmth of the flames and their nurturing quality as you witness purification over time. This should feel good and calming to you!
- Be patient with yourself as you do this for the first time; you might have to move through some emotional material that has been stored in the pelvis and that is now given a way to clear itself.
- Give it the time it takes. Trust the process. It will get better and more enjoyable each time you go back to it. You are cultivating a stronger, more resilient second chakra.

Third Chakra

A healthy third chakra has your vital organs humming in harmony with each other, supporting good digestion, a healthy sense of belonging, cooperation, and contribution. All this is expressed through the positive and natural personal power of your unique individuality. The quality of your thoughts is governed by this chakra, as are your belief systems and sense of human truth.

Any complaints in the organs governed by the third chakra, like the liver, gallbladder, stomach, pancreas, spleen, and small intestine, can be traced back to a malfunctioning third chakra. Generally, this center is overused and abused as we push forward with too much mental energy fueled by coffee and sugary drinks to gear up for the task, while alternately trying to calm an overworked system with too many carbohydrates, meats, alcohol, and more sugary treats.

Tears in the grid covering the individual layers of the third chakra are common, resulting in an energy leak and making digestion problematic. A congested liver may cloud the thinking with negative tendencies and a difficulty when it comes to letting go, as a broken record of unwanted negative thoughts and feelings may steal the show of what could be an otherwise enjoyable day.

When the third center is functioning well, we tend to enjoy our uniqueness with confidence while appreciating the same in others. We know what is ours to give and contribute from our wholeness to those around us. When out of balance we either overpower with a sense of an overblown ego personality, or we might shrink away from challenges because of a lack of confidence. As our inner conversation wallpapers our daily thoughts, unchecked negative mental framing will cause digestive erosion, with too much acidity literally burning holes into the stomach lining. Mental hygiene proves itself most beneficial here, helping to weed out thoughts of defeat and revenge as we choose to live in positive reality. Outdated belief systems based on trauma are dissolved and replaced with life-affirming thoughts of choice, in harmony with the self and others.

Exercise to Begin Clearing your Third Chakra

Give yourself ten minutes for this exercise. Sit and breathe naturally into the area of your solar plexus. If you have disturbances or complaints in your third chakra area, to begin with, feel into it in detail. Where exactly to you feel the energy leak or disturbance in your body? Notice if the feeling is predominantly physical, emotional, or mental.

- The statement is, "I allow it."
- Then with your eyes closed, focus on the area specifically where you feel a disturbance; stay present to yourself right in this area. Listen to your body. Ask yourself, What is needed here? Are there any foods that I am eating that are not benefiting me? And what are they?
- What comes to mind after you ask that question? What do you see or think of?
- You can also ask yourself, What foods that I am eating presently no longer serve my health and well-being at this point?
- What is the emotion that is present as you feel into this area? Do you feel anger, fear, or resentment? And if so, who is this inner dispute with? What needs to be communicated, forgiven, and let go of?
- When you listen to inner dialogue, is it self-supporting or is it tearing you down? Can you be your own inner best friend while talking to yourself internally?
- Remember that you're whole and complete in your own right already. Letting go of trauma is a process. Be gentle and kind in your inner conversation with yourself.
- Before you get up, please say, "I honor and celebrate my unique individuality!" It is your closing statement for this exercise! How does it make you feel to say this?

The Heart Chakra (aka the Fourth Chakra): It's All About Love

The heart chakra is all about love, giving, receiving, and being. It regulates how we relate to the world around us, our loved ones, family, friends, animals, nature, and creation at large. The heart chakra connects us to the truth of our being in time and eternity, as well as to our more distant past and to who and what we have been in other life times.

The fastest way to heal the heart chakra is through forgiveness.

The heart has the unique ability to record and remember key events beyond this life both positive and traumatic. Positive lifetime events integrate and get carried forward naturally and are seen as God-given talents or blessings in present life. Traumatic events that left a scarring on the spiritual, mental, emotional, and physical body are equally recorded and are often labeled chronic this time around.

The heart is the gateway into the quantum reality of the multidimensional nature that is our true being.

The heart chakra in the front governs our physical heart, the lungs, the thymus, and also the longing for our soul's fulfillment. The back of the heart chakra has everything to do with our willingness to see the world as a loving place for who we are, uniquely. If it is open, we tend to feel loved and accepted as who we are. If one feels victimized or betrayed as a norm, meaning this feeling is a repetitive theme in this life, then most likely, this chakra is closed, blocked, or distorted. Chronic pain in the upper back or shoulder blades is symptom of a blocked or closed heart chakra in the back.

The heart connects us to our emotional feeling body and is intimately related to the second and sixth chakra (third eye), all of which are love chakras.

Like any other chakra, the heart chakra can open or close. If desired, it can evolve over time into a beautiful flowering that will affect all areas of one's life in the most positive healing way. Being willing to forgive the grievances we hold against others is key.

Conversely, the heart can be trained to hold down and stagnate by repeated negative mental framing, which will result in literally sucking the joy out of life. A telltale of a closed heart is continued relentless criticism of others or the world, usually combined with a lamenting of one's own reality.

When the heart chakra is open, we are open to life, love, and creation. Then we are positive in attitude and being, allowing assistance and offering a hand to others in need. Healing is greatly accelerated when the heart moves from a closed to an open state. It is much more difficult, if not impossible, to fully heal without the assistance of our spiritual being, which we access through our heart. Many afflictions are based in very old traumas of the distant past (as in past lives) that can only be reached through the doorway of the heart. Without the awareness and assistance of our greater spiritual being, the healing process will surely be stifled.

But miracles happen when the heart opens with compassion and forgiveness. Instantly, ancient traumas are released, including intense physical pain, which often disappears within seconds.

Exercise to Clear and Heal the Heart Chakra

Take at least ten minutes. Sit and focus on the natural flow of breath in the center of your chest.

- The statement is, "I am love."
- Then, keeping your focus on the center of your chest, connect with the natural ebb and flow of your breath. What do you feel here?
- Are you experiencing joy or sadness when you focus at the center of your chest?
  Do you feel bright and energized or a sense of dullness? Whatever it is, allow it!
- What persons come to mind as you do this? What is the story or issue that arises? Is there someone or something that needs to be forgiven? If you are present to blame or anger against someone or even yourself, it's a sign that forgiveness is needed.
- To forgive, say, "It is my choice to forgive [name of person (for example, my mother)] completely for [name what happened (for example, abandoning me when ....)]. I forgive [her or him], as well as life, God, myself, and nature now, completely. And that is my choice now! Thank you."
- Then sit and wait a few minutes for things to clear. Each person or incident requires a separate statement.

For best results do one incident or one person at the time. Pushing yourself to go faster does not increase results. However, being kind and gentle to yourself does make for best results.

The Fifth Chakra (the Throat Chakra)

The fifth chakra, also known as the throat chakra, governs our will, as well as our relationship with divine will. The fifth chakra is quite complex and has many functions. Physically, the front aspect governs the thyroid, throat, voice box, and upper esophagus, while the back aspect governs the cervical spine.

How we use language to speak our reality into being determines, in part, the state and health of the fifth chakra. It is the negotiating link between heart and head and serves to balance our will with divine will and the greater good for all. Our relationship with authority is reflected in the use of the fifth chakra, as well as how we relate to others and ourselves.

Common issues with the fifth chakra include thyroid problems, neck pain or stiffness, any kind of throat complaints, difficulty swallowing, or vocal expression.

A blocked fifth chakra might keep us from expressing our feelings, preventing us from voicing our wants and needs and, therefore, creating an inability to receive. Hence, one might be living in a state of self-perpetuated lack. Being able to voice our wants and needs is the first step to receiving.

Ask and you shall receive. Even in spiritual reality, this holds true, as there will be no interference with our free will. A request for guidance or help from the MDST has to be stated, clearly, in order to be fulfilled. Otherwise, it would be a break in universal law, *the law of free will*. It is important to state here, that *a complaint is not a request*. We all either have done this ourselves or know someone who just loves to complain and then complains about the fact that there seems to be no help.

The motto of the fifth chakra is ask and you shall receive! For our multidimensional support team to step in and provide the help that is desired, it has to be requested. Better yet, the request should be stated in a clear and specific way, with a thank you on the end. That ensures there can be no doubt about our willingness to receive what we have asked for.

The fifth chakra allows us to communicate with and participate in divine will. By aligning our will with divine will, we come to serve the greater good for all. In turn, we are being served in the very best and most elegant way possible. The right use of the fifth chakra creates a win-win situation that is often so surprisingly simple and elegant that it might seem like magic.

The fifth chakra is the center of divine truth, the third chakra human truth, and the first chakra physical truth.

When the throat chakra is functioning well, we tend to use our voice in alignment with our creative longing, feeling calm, cool, and collected, while being aware of (and participating in) a network support system that serves the greater good of all. Those in teaching and leading positions usually have well-formed throat chakras.

Exercise to Begin Healing Your Fifth Chakra, or Throat Chakra

- Take at least ten minutes. Sit for a few moments in silence, breathing naturally while tuning into your throat chakra.
- The statement is, I align my will with divine will.
- Physically, how is the area around your throat feeling? Does it feel open or blocked in someway?
- Do you express yourself easily? Or are you hesitant or shy?
- Generally, are you speaking your truth? Or are you holding back?
- What is the quality of your communication like, with others, with source, and with yourself?
- How do you speak your creation into being?
- How easy is it for you to ask for help?

- If there is one thing that needs to be expressed now, what is it and to whom? If there is one thing that you need help with in your life right now, who can you ask?
- To invite spiritual guidance and assistance, try this. Say, "It is my choice and my request for guidance and help in this matter. [State the issue in brief.] I give thanks for any and all help, your guidance and assistance. Thank you!"
- Then sit and let it go. You may receive some information right away or in the next hour or day. Trust the process.

The motto of the fifth chakra is "ask and you shall receive." But remember, first one has to ask in order to receive.

The Sixth Chakra (the Third Eye)

The sixth chakra, aka the third eye, connects us to our inner and outer vision. It is how we project our personal and unique vision onto the great screen of life. The third eye governs the left eye, the pituitary, the frontal lobe of the brain, and our thinking. It's about perception, evaluating, and decision making. The sixth chakra is also a love center connecting us to our divine and even celestial nature. Here we look to beauty, nature, poetry, art, and music to enrich our lives and create a doorway to experience a greater than human universal love. Remember the last time you were awed by the magnificence of nature or touched by a particularly beautiful piece of music or poetry? Did it not lift you out of ordinary consciousness into an experience of greater reality, connecting you to God or source?

The sixth chakra is the lens through which we view life, and it is also the lens through which we are projecting our vision onto the screen of life. Perpetual fear-based thinking will distort the sixth chakra over time. A prolonged lack of beauty in our lives can also weaken the sixth chakra. Being in nature and enjoying flowers, trees, sunsets, and looking into the eyes of a loved one can elevate an ordinary moment into a blessed event—reminding us of our own divine nature. Music, poetry, and art are also sixth chakra superfoods that can nurture your third eye into more wholeness and greater functionality.

The sixth chakra, or third eye, is a lens and a doorway, allowing us to see beyond the normal realm of vision into other dimensions and even into the inner structure of our own human anatomy, depending on how we focus the lens of our third eye. Think of a microscope and how it can be adjusted to focus on different levels of depth and magnification; our sixth chakra functions in much the same way. Divine intuition is another important aspect of the sixth chakra, as in being able to see events before they occur. This intuition may be experienced in dreams or meditative visions.

When the sixth chakra is closed or distorted, our thinking is not clear, and we may be chronically indecisive. By not being able to see the option of an elegant solution, we may go for the tried and (not so) true limiting choice. With an open, fully integrated third eye, we can connect to the bigger picture and even feel the magic in our life.

The front of the sixth chakra is an ultimately creative chakra, as it guides decision making, how we view our experience, and what we decide to focus and project onto the screen of life. *The back of the sixth* helps to make it happen, providing the will and staying power behind the vision. We all know someone who is full of good ideas but not able to execute the vision in reality. The telltale sign of a chronically closed sixth chakra, the one in the back of the head, is plenty of pie-in-the sky vision without manifestation. It is the person who talks endlessly about this and that project but never seems to manifest any of them.

By claiming our sixth chakra, we can redirect our life to a desired vista that is in alignment with our greater purpose and the joy and fulfillment that is the promise of our life.

Exercise to Claim Your Sixth Chakra

- Take at least ten minutes for this meditation.
- The statement is, "I am divinely loved and guided."
- To begin, sit and observe your natural breath for a few moments.
- Then shift your focus to your third eye between your brows and the center of your head in line with your ears.
- Notice, how does this area of your sixth chakra feel? Does it feel clear, or foggy, blocked, or jumbled? How does the back of your head feel?
- What are you envisioning for your life?
- Is what you are projecting onto the screen of your life in alignment with your longing? And do your daily actions match it? In other words, do you support your vision by moving into action and putting in motion and manifesting the life you desire?
- Now in order to claim more of your sixth chakra function, visualize yourself—a very small version of your essence self (all the best parts of yourself)—sitting inside the center of your own head on a golden lotus flower. Here, you are in charge of your thoughts and of directing your life. Keep breathing and imagine light radiating from your essence self, filling your head with light.
- Sit until you feel clear enough and then ask yourself this question: What is the next step in realizing my vision?
- Be willing to receive information on that next step. You only have to know your next step to move forward. When this step is in motion in your life, ask for the next step to fulfilling your vision.
- Know that you are guided, divinely loved, and divinely supported in fulfilling your vision.

The Seventh Chakra

The seventh chakra is our energetic halo at the top of the head. It is the biggest, most complex chakra connecting us to all that is, was, and ever will be. It opens us to our creative God consciousness, as expressed through our unique individuality. It is activated when we are participating fully as creative God beings in the ultimate mystery of life. The seventh chakra is the crowning glory through which knowledge, insight, and wisdom are imparted directly and in detail. This knowledge and wisdom go beyond intellectual knowing. It is here that we can reach into the unlimited God realm, or source of all, receiving that which we need to know and share in order to serve the greater good for all.

Here *the divine genius of all* interacts with the *divine genius of our unique individuality*, giving us brilliant insights and helping us to solve complex problems in the most elegant and efficient ways. Revolutionary new technological inventions are pulled straight from the unified field by the seventh chakra. Such inventions have a chance of being made real when the individual pulling them from this field is fully connected all throughout the field and body.

Think of the great inventions of our time and the individuals behind them. Some of the recent greats that come to my mind are Tesla and Elon Musk, Steve Jobs, Bill Gates, Mark Zuckerman, Oprah, and Dr. Barbara Ann Brennan. When the seventh chakra is fully integrated and reaches deep down into physical reality by connecting with its counterpart, the first chakra, we are able to create heaven on earth. This is the ultimate promise of the seventh chakra—to make real the dream of heaven on earth, to make life good and right for everyone.

With a blocked or closed seventh chakra, we may be cut off from our inner and outer divine genius. Unable to connect to the God-given greatness of our true nature, we may feel disconnected from source and not clear as to our purpose.

Physically, the seventh chakra governs the brain, the pineal gland, the nervous system, and the right eye. (The left eye is governed by the sixth chakra.)

Exercise to Open, Clear, and Expand Your Seventh Chakra

- The statement is, "I am a vital part of all that is."
- Sit for about ten minutes (with a straight back if you can).
- Visualize the earth underneath your feet (no matter where you are).
- Breathing naturally, visualize and feel earth energy come up through your feet and legs into your pelvis, up to your heart, and through your neck. Feel and see it expanding into a spiral out the top of your head.
- Stay firmly grounded even as you open to the vastness of the universe through your seventh chakra.
- The first chakra is the counterpart to the seventh chakra. Feel the grounding support of the earth as you open to the expanding consciousness of your seventh chakra, connecting you to all that is—which you are an integral part of—the whole mystery of life. You are connected to and part of the all of it!
- Feel the uniqueness of your being in connection with all that is. Soak it up.

Chapter 5

THE ART OF RESTING AND RECEIVING

Your body has something in the neighborhood of 40 trillion cells, quite a consulting committee. Call on it when you're confused or undecided. Relax quietly and ask your body what it has to say.

—Victoria Moran

Resting is an integral and essential part of any self-healing practice. Connecting to your aura and your chakra system can be difficult at times, especially for the beginner. Exhaustion or tiredness will also affect one's ability to focus. Resting for healing is a skill and an art. When mastered, it will advance the health of your aura.

In order to heal, we need to rest and pay attention to our feedback systems. Our physical body, in combination with the aura, is a self-healing organism. Given the right condition, it will heal by balancing itself. All humans have a God-given ability to heal themselves. Often just a little rest is needed to do the trick, provided the balancing system is functioning, which means you are listening to the messages your body is giving you.

Your body is the vehicle through which you express who you are—mind, heart, and soul. It is your soul's physical embodiment!

It will tell you what you need and when but one has to (or has to learn to) listen.

Most of us push ourselves too much and too far. We don't notice the red light sending us the message to rest. We just keep going on and on, until finally, we are exhausted and collapse. *Then* we feel it is justified—maybe—to rest. Often, by that time, the switch is stuck in the "on" position. And with all that mental activity, we *think* we can't get off the treadmill. Despite the fact that we are exhausted, the mind keeps going on a merry-go-round. "I can't stop now. I have to do this. And this. Otherwise, there will be hell to pay"—and so on. This is a reaction from an unbalanced system and an internal call for help, letting us know that we are stuck. You know the story well. It's a vicious cycle until you are finally on your back—forced to take a rest.

Disease can happen when we are busy ignoring the signs of an advancing condition. We numb ourselves to the telltale signs that signal, "I am tired and need rest." And in doing so, we might keep ourselves going with copious amounts of coffee, perhaps followed by sleeping pills to get some shut-eye when the tasks are finally done. By ignoring the need for rest, overriding the prompt of the body, and pushing forward with caffeinated willpower we are likely to damage our first chakra over time, thereby inviting disease. Separating will and body, the willful mind is now infected by the collective push to accomplish more, to do more, and therefore to get more, believing this is somehow better. Fear is also a driving factor. What if I don't have enough? The monkey mind holds the will hostage against the body, telling it, "You can rest when I am done with you and all my tasks"—until finally, exhaustion creates an even deeper crisis.

Almost always, when someone is in this particular cycle, the first chakra is damaged and out of kilter. But other energy centers are involved as well. The person invariably has lost touch with his or her body and its feedback system. Rest then becomes like an old friend in the long gone past, difficult to remember and not easy to get back in touch with.

The problem is that we confuse our system with conflicting

demands and commands. This ultimately leads to the eventual breakdown in the system. We receive the message from the body to rest, eat, or move because it is trying to help us rebalance and get back on track. It does not serve us to ignore the signs or treat it as a bother or something to get rid of. When we ignore the feedback system of our physical body, overriding it with will power of the mind, we may lose track of the body and what it needs. Over time, with repetitive stress, physical vitality gives way to a feeling of dullness and exhaustion. The system is now compromised, no longer recharging but struggling to keep up.

Resting plays an essential part in the rhythm of life, just as silence is an essential part of music. Every person has an individual need for rest, which may change according to what is going on in one's life. When we are in a creative cycle, we are energized by creativity and might need a minimum of rest. At the end of a creative cycle, when all has been spent, the need for rest increases again.

Resting allows one to move forward with vigor and renewed creativity. In times of illness, rest will help our bodies recover and provide an opportunity to deepen the connection with the energetic layers of the field. Then we will be able to hear and respond to the messages the body is signaling. There may be an aha moment waiting to happen, initiating an entirely new path of healing and creative expression. Rest is beautiful when one finally surrenders to it. It can take you deep into your inner core to help bring forth aspects of yourself that have been waiting and wanting to emerge, hence making your life more whole. A feeling of wholeness means healing has been accomplished!

The best way to get back to resting is to exercise the body and tire it out with a brisk walk, yoga, or any other chosen exercise. Follow the exercise with horizontal positioning, like the resting pose at the end of a yoga session, and rest deeply. Keep your mind on your breath and track the sensations of your body for as long as you can. This helps you stay off the mindless merry-go-round of your thoughts, even though they disguise themselves as important. Let go of your thoughts completely for ten to fifteen minutes. That means don't react by going on that train of thought. Let the thought pass you by like clouds, while focusing on your breath. When you get back to it, it may be all in balance and for your greater good! You don't have to go to sleep (every time) in order to rest. One can learn to rest deeply (supplementing nighttime sleep) and get great results that will carry you through the day with grace and ease.

Healing Skill: Statement for a Deep Healing Rest

- Before you initiate a healing rest, decide how much time you have—thirty minutes, forty-five minutes, or an hour. Set a timer if you like.
- Make sure that you are undisturbed during this time and that your body is most comfortable. Support your neck and lower back in a way that feels best to you. Try a pillow underneath your knees to support you lower back and a smaller one for your neck.
- Turn off your phone!
- Then lie on your back and read the following invocation out loud.
- I [your name] declare this a sacred space for a healing for myself.

     I ask for truth, love, and healing on all levels of being and, in particular, for this issue at hand.

     [State the issue.] (To begin with you might ask for a nourishing twenty-minute nap that has you feeling refreshed and inspired. It's best to start out simple so that you can track your experience and then graduate to more complex healings.)

     I ask for the highest level of healing, and I give thanks for the healing I am about to receive.

     I welcome and invite assistance and guidance in relationship to the issue at hand.

I give thanks for the presence of my multidimensional support team and for their presence, guidance, and assistance.

I turn the healing over to the Holy Spirit for the greater good of all.

And so it is. It is done. Thank you. Amen!

The more you use this invocation, the better it will work. And practice makes perfect. Requesting, commanding, and receiving your own healing is an art and a skill that is refined over time. Personally, I have used this simple invocation for all the years that I have been practicing. It has handed me the keys to the kingdom that is my health and my life.

Healing Skill: The Art of Receiving

The art of receiving is a healing skill in and of itself. If you practice it as a skill, you will be able to refine it to an art. There is no successful art without pleasure. Enjoyment of the process is the key to your success in healing.

When receiving a self-healing, accept that your healing is under way as soon as you initiate it. Choose to receive it fully. It works best when you make it a conscious choice by saying it out loud. Say, "It is my choice to relax deeply and to receive this healing that is coming my way now. And that is my choice!"

Then connect to the pleasure current of your breath. Doing so means observing the effortless ebb and flow of your breath. There is nothing that you have to do other than to observe your breath. Life is breathing you. Enjoy.

What does it feel like to receive your breath, through your nose and mouth, down through the airways, and into your lungs, inflating them? Do you enjoy the way it feels when the oxygenated blood circulates, nurturing your organs, limbs, and brain? What is it like for you to know you are being cared for in in this simple but extraordinary way? You might not feel much at first, but subtle sensations, tingling, and perhaps emotions may surface. It all depends on what your healing is about—what you have requested and initiated.

Let go and enjoy the journey. Each healing is unique and will take you to a slightly different place. You may go to sleep or into a state of deep relaxation as soon as you initiate. At other times, you might be acutely aware and present to the changes occurring in you body and your field. Healing sessions are accumulative and will advance your ability to receive as you are fine-tuning your aura progressively over time.

Chapter 6

THE MULTIDIMENSIONAL SUPPORT TEAM

Only divine love bestows the keys of knowledge.

—Arthur Rimbaud

The healing that I receive and practice with my clients and myself would not be possible without my multidimensional support team, my MDST. In this chapter I will give you a detailed look at how I came to assemble my MDST, or how it enlisted me. It happened over the course of thirty years, and my team is still growing.

What is a MDST? It is a team of beings made up of deities, spirit guides, spirit surgeons, angelic beings, ascended masters, and other humans who are embodied or not. They are living light aspects of God, or the unlimited source from which all things spring forth, and they are in service to humanity. Every person who works in support of the greater good of all has a team available. The more extensive your task, the bigger your team! It is safe to say that all leaders, teachers, and doctors have guides, even if they don't know it (or perhaps don't even believe in them). If you have a job in the service of others and for the greater good for all, you have divine guidance available to you. As a matter fact, divine guidance is available to all who ask for it. Ask and you shall receive is a true statement and the motto of the fifth chakra through which divine guidance enters the field.

Getting to Know My Team: The Early Years

I am now going to take you on a journey of my early team, when I didn't know that I had one. It is only in looking back that I gather the gist of all that had to fall into place for me to become who I am. I can now see the golden thread that was weaving it all together, even when I was twelve years old. This includes a pastor who, it seems maliciously and ignorantly, handed me what I can now see and appreciate as a dark gift.

My first encounter with a member of my MDST was Jesus Christ. As a child, every Sunday, my late brother and I walked hand in hand to church. Dressed in our Sunday best, we would make the trek from our house down to the old town church. It was a Lutheran church, and the pastor knew our whole family. One day, Pastor Lichtenstein asked my brother and myself to come to the altar. Thinking we had done something bad or wrong and a little afraid, we both stepped forward, anticipating a scolding. But we got flowers instead, straight from the altar. We were honored for our regular attendance and for the fact that, every week, we made the long walk from our neighborhood down to church.

The Dark Gift

Six years later, while preparing for my confirmation, the Lutheran ritual affirmation of baptism, I was attending my weekly yearlong class for confirmation the following year. I asked the usual questions about God; Christ; and why war, suffering, and children starving were allowed to exist. Pastor Lichtenstein did not answer. He passed me over and ignored me, not ever addressing my question. I was very puzzled over this, and it bothered me that my questions did not get addressed, no matter how often I put my hand up and kept it up. Pastor Lichtenstein never called on me again. I took the matter of confirmation quite seriously and, after thinking about it for some time, decided that I could not go ahead with the matter, based on the fact that I did not know what I was getting confirmed in (what the confirmation represented). I suspect my parents did not object because it saved them time and money. They did not try to convince me otherwise, and I never went back to confirmation class.

Weeks after that, I saw the pastor with his two young sons in the town square. Walking up to him, I put my hand out in a greeting, wanting to say hello. But he did not reach for my hand. Ignoring my gesture and puffing his chest, he told me that he did not know me and turned away. I was dumbfounded, in disbelief over what had just happened. Walking home, I felt something shatter in me. Was he not supposed to be kind and compassionate? Why was he turning away from me? Was my termination of confirmation class cause for such rejection and annihilation? I felt badly. Had I done wrong? No matter what, I felt more alone than ever. And with that, I was plunged into deep teen darkness, questioning my existence, the good of God, and myself. Now there was no one, not even God to turn to.

I had so many questions, and with no one to talk to, I would send them out to the universe at night when I could not sleep. Is there a God? What is of God? Does time end? What happens after I die? Do I matter? Does God know me? Listen to me? Are there other beings, other than humans? Do I end at my fingertips? How come I cannot find the end of it all when I go out into the universe? Would God give us eyes to see and a mind to comprehend the whole of eternity, only to give humans a life span that seems like a blink of an eye of about eighty-five years to then have our lives terminated and possibly commit us to hell? That would truly be cruel.

I turned these questions over and over, and the first thing that became clear to me was that I had a consciousness that could not be extinguished by death! And if there was a God, I would know myself as that—as we are made in "his" likeness according to the Bible. That made sense to me; *direct access to God* was the only thing that made sense to me. I also had a knowing, an understanding, about telepathic communication and that love was key and fear was mostly a self-fulfilling prophecy.

My First Direct Contact

In my early thirties, I had a direct and conscious experience of the Christ energy. One afternoon while relaxing on my bed and musing on life in general, in my small nunlike quarters, a tiny studio apartment in the foothills above the Santa Barbara Mission, I became aware of a warm and pleasant sensation in my chest and heart. I instinctively recognized it to be Christ's compassion, even though I had never felt it before. It was distinct, personal, warm, loving, and physically real.

Before that moment, Christ's energy was an idea of the mind. Opening to it, I connected to the Christ heart—the great compassion within me. This compassion I felt was not just for "the other"; it included myself I knew in that moment that I was part of that divine love. Now looking back at my timeline, this occurrence fits beautifully into the unfolding destiny of my healer's journey. However gentle, it was a significant opening in my life, connecting me directly with Christ consciousness through my own heart. As I was able to fully accept the experience, it initiated me instantly into higher vibrational signature.

Getting Hooked Up

Over the years, I had other openings and introductions to deities, ascended masters, angels, and spirit guides. They occurred naturally, different but similar in presentation, making themselves available to me and (as I now realize) becoming a part of my MDST.

I was introduced to Saint Germain while learning to meditate. I had read *Unveiled Mysteries* by Godfrey Ray King and was taken by the nobility of Saint Germain. The ascended master is the ambassador of true freedom, sacred abundance, and the I

Am presence. Unless something made absolute sense to me, I would not, could not adhere to it. The I Am presence made a lot of sense to me, right down to the correct use of language and being in right relationship to abundant resources. It put everything into perspective and connected me with the possibility of personal freedom.

I sat at 4:00 a.m. every morning for a half a year, determined to learn and master the art of meditation. With the help of Saint Germain, I unraveled the negative patterning of my mind, replacing old patterns with positive, creative thoughts. Many mornings, while squirming in my skin, old accumulated nonspecific but uncomfortable and frustrated feelings were unwinding, ready to be let go from my body and soul. I knew Saint Germain to be close by. I knew I was making progress right from the get-go because, no matter how difficult or frustrating a meditation was, sleep afterward was a little more heavenly—so much so that I was looking forward it. Meditation helped me unwind, relax my mind, and dream more consciously, which in turn enhanced my sleep.

Claiming my innate wisdom, discovering the body-mind connection, I directed my mind to support my task. For example, I discovered that, if I harmonized my mind in alignment with meditation, it would serve me right. My thoughts no longer frustrated me but offered up a new experience. Now, I focused my thoughts and observations in harmony with the process of meditation by observing my breath, for example. As I began to harmonize with all aspects of it, soon the practice of sitting became enjoyable. In meditation, I got to be with myself, feel my feelings, hear myself, sense my body, and listen to my heart. Tuning my inner compass in the direction of my true north, I adjusted to the fulfillment of my purpose.

Down to My Knees

That doesn't mean all was suddenly happiness and apple pie. On the contrary, everything that did not work got stripped away, collapsing the outer scaffolding of my life's details, shortly after I began to meditate. No doubt, a necessary course correction was taking place. I was thirty-four years old. A love relationship had just ended, and a business alliance that had proved itself to be a mirage left me without home, car, or viable means of supporting myself. With a few hundred dollars left to my name and staying with a friend, I was on countdown. I needed to find work before my money ran out. I held my head above water for a few weeks, and then I was down to my last hundred-dollar bill. The day I broke the remaining Ben Franklin, I fell apart. I went to my knees crying and prayed to my father in heaven, my actual father who had died in previous months. I knew that my father's consciousness was alive and well. His spirit had come to me after his passing to let me know specifically that he would be my father in heaven for a time.

So now was the time, and I prayed like never before. Feeling relieved that I did not have to pray to a God whose existence I doubted, I prayed to my to my biological father in heaven (or the ethers), and I made a very specific request. I asked him to assist me in finding the kind of work opportunity that would utilize and make good on my natural gifts—a mutually beneficial exchange that would help me grow into more of who I was meant to be. I also asked to be reimbursed at face value. I surprised myself with the focus of my intention. I felt it physically and in my heart. I will never forget the laser-sharp focused intention I put behind that prayer. I don't ever remember being that specific about anything, before that particular moment. But I knew when I prayed that my life depended on it. I felt it in my bones. There was a certainty in my request and a readiness to receive it. It truly became the doorway to the rest of my life.

Within hours, my ex-boyfriend called. Alarmed by the obviously stressed tone of my voice, he asked me, "What's wrong?"

While sobbing, I related my situation. After listening intently, Charlie said he knew of an opening at a health and fitness spa. He thought it might be a fit for me and said that he would make the call.

Within less than twelve hours, I was connected to my new job opportunity, which ultimately proved to be the key to the rest of my life. It was exactly what I had asked for, no less! I knew that my prayer had been answered and that my father had kept true to his promise. He was most certainly on my team.

The job that was offered to me was my dream job. Indeed, I got to contribute my natural and acquired talents. I was to be a fitness guide at the Ashram Spa and Health Retreat, a well-known boot camp spa experience located in Calabasas, California. I was to start as a massage therapist and then move positions when another fitness trainer was leaving. I was to start immediately.

The Golden Gift

After several months of working as a massage therapist, I moved on to assume my position as a fitness instructor. My first week on the job, I met a very kind, most interesting, eccentric, and wealthy man, who was a guest at the spa. We had an instant connection. Walking together on hikes, we enjoyed long conversations. And throughout his stay at the spa, we became fast friends. At the end of the week, he left me a $1,000 tip included in a personal letter to me, making sure that I would not forget him. Surprised but grateful for the generous gift, I gave him a heartfelt hug and thanked him at his departure. We exchanged contact information and promised to be in touch.

Norman was a godsend, a true mensch. His friendship would come to mean the world to me, and he remains a dear friend to this day. I remember feeling something in Norman's presence I had not experienced before, an undeniable recognition of another soul. Somehow I knew that this soft-spoken, mild-mannered eccentric who was fifteen years my senior held the key to my kingdom. It turns out that he is the reason I was able to embrace my purpose with relative ease and grace.

I knew that I could count on Norman to be there at a moment's notice but was always surprised to get him by phone without delay. Even so, our contact was sporadic in the beginning. A phone call or the occasional letter would let me know his presence in my life was not fleeting but that of a real friend.

After two years of friendship, my heart awakened. Vivid night dreams of a romantic connection made champagne bubbles rise in my heart, with the future casting a happy shadow of love divine into my sleep. Soon after, Norman invited me to spend a long weekend at his house up the coast, south of San Francisco. I accepted his invitation and got on a plane the week after Thanksgiving. When I arrived, I was amazed to find his house filled with flowers. Every corner of his home was adorned with that elegant, delicate, and playful essence that is the flower's grace. All my friends know that I have a great love and weakness for the flower kingdom, rendering me defenseless against such beauty. And thus, being in the home of my dear friend, I was touched forever by the beauty and depth of his soul. I remember it as the moment I fell in love with Norman.

In many ways, Norman and I made an unlikely couple. Given our age difference, lifestyles, and habits, we would never have met if not for my job at the Ashram Spa and Health Retreat. Over time, I came to understand that our relationship was determined by our individual purpose, and in support for the greater good of all.

A year into our relationship, I took a workshop, Poetry in Motion, with the now late Emily Conrad, the founder of the Continuum Movement and author of *Life on Land*. It was a rare opportunity to immerse myself in the Continuum Movement for a whole week while fueling the flow of writing poetry. It was to be my first official introduction to writing. For me, at the time, it was an altogether scary undertaking, as an early childhood trauma terrorized me every time I had to pick up a pen and write in public. Thus, I froze if there was somebody around to observe me writing. Unable to remember how to spell the simplest words, cringing in embarrassment, I would fall apart. Therefore, writing in public was to be avoided under any circumstance, and yet I was determined to challenge this debilitating trauma.

Hesitant but armed with colored pencils and a very big paper drawing block, I made my way to class. What came to pass was an unexpected and quite liberating experience. With Emily Conrad's brilliant guidance in her movement work and a guest teacher sporting a PhD in literature, I went on a weeklong writing adventure that changed my life. I found myself writhing on the floor, moving my body in unrestricted, weird, and wonderfully strange ways that is the signature of the Continuum Movement, which looks much like an amoeba in motion. While I was crawling on the floor, inspiration wiggled out of me, spilling fully formed poems onto paper. I was surprised to find beautifully written masterpieces flowing out me that needed no editing, which earned me praise from Emily and the PhD in literature. When I shared them later with Norman, they also proved to be the ticket to my future. Norman was so moved and impressed by what I had written that he decided to give me my own personal MacArthur Grant—a two-year stipend to cover all my living expenses and then some. It was a small fortune indeed and a gift that would change the course of my life.

The original MacArthur Fellowship, also called "Genius Grant" is usually a five-year grant to individuals who show exceptional creativity in their work and the prospect for still more in the future. The fellowship is designed to provide recipients with the flexibility to pursue their artistic, intellectual, and professional activities in the absence of specific obligations or reporting requirements. There are no limits on age or area of activity. That was when I knew that writing was in my future and that I was, in fact, a writer.

The Black Velvet Void

Norman's gift of the MacArthur Grant gave me two years of unrestricted freedom to explore my creativity and what would come next. I quit my job at the ashram to become familiar with what many refer to as "the burden and responsibility of freedom." Now I had two years to spend as I wished, and I had to make it count. Failure was not an option. I had to move myself forward to new and higher ground.

One might think that the prospect of two years paid leave equals carefree happiness. Well it didn't. I took the plunge into freedom and landed square on my butt, in the dark velvet void. The void is the place absent of the comfort of what is known; it is the pure, empty dark velvet space that holds within itself all possibilities, waiting to be discovered and created.

It was a strange experience to have the kind of freedom, time, and money that everyone dreams about and to be faced with the true responsibility of it. What was I going to do with my time to make it count? Days, weeks, and months spread out in front of me almost glaringly. I had to remind myself of how fortunate I was to keep from sinking into despair. I also adopted a chop-wood, carry-water attitude that had me exercising daily, attending yoga classes, going on wonderful hikes, keeping house, and caring for myself to the best of my knowledge. I frequented the farmers market, prepared nutritious meals, read, painted, shopped, and enjoyed time with my friends and traveling with Norman.

A year into my sabbatical, I became aware of an internal pressure, the squeeze of the void upon my outer membrane. Either I was growing or the space around me was getting smaller. I felt increasingly uncomfortable in my skin, knowing I had gone past the halfway mark of my granted time with no new vision of my life on the horizon. Then one evening while browsing a new age bookstore a familiar book lit up in front of me. It was a book on the function and healing power of the human aura, *Hands of Light* by Barbara Ann Brennan.

I had read it seven years earlier and all but devoured it. I recognized the truth it conveyed as part of my own life's work. I had read it cover to cover in one weekend, so excited by what I found that I couldn't put it down until I had absorbed it all. However, I had become very depressed right after I'd finished reading it. Here it was, right in my hands, the manual I had been looking for all my life, answering my questions and filling in missing links. It is addressed my questions about who and what we are as humans and about the direct link to God or the divine. *Hands of Light* answered questions that had been occupying my mind for as long as I could remember. But with no money to my name to pay for four years tuition and travel expenses, the promise this book offered—to allow me to explore its answers more deeply in a program based on its concepts—was impossible.

A feeling of depression set in as I realized I had no means to attend the four-year program, Healing Science, on the East Coast. However, I had a very strong desire and a distinct physical knowing (in my bones) that it would be part of my future. Seven years ago I had put my dream aside, promising myself to find a way to study what my heart so desired. Now here it was back in my hands with Norman by my side, and I instantly knew what I needed to do. The seed that had been nurtured in the dark velvet void and warmed by the invisible sun had germinated and sprouted a leaf—one that was yet in the ground.

My excitement and decision to attend the program was met and supported with incredible generosity by Norman. His offer to pay my four years of tuition and travel expenses in full singlehandedly helped me fulfill a dream seven years in the making. I was over the moon and crying tears of joy while filling out my application for the Brennan Healing Science School.

So, here is a heartfelt thanks to my early team, including the pastor, who gave me the dark gift of rejection so that I could find my own way to God and source. I now herewith forgive you, Pastor Lichtenstein. I lay down the burden of blame and rejection, knowing I have found my way and that nothing was taken from me that was truly mine. I give thanks to my wonderful friend Norman. You heeded the call of your inner voice to help me find my way. Thank you for providing the space and the resources that allowed me to claim my gift and for the freedom that is my life.

Initiation

The Brennan Healing Science School initiated me into a new depth of personal healing, as well as into my healer-ship. It was where I opened to myself and began to understand who and what I am. I discovered myself to be a natural when it came to connecting to the spiritual and subtle energetic world.

These realms are not just esoteric ideas, and I now know with certainty that our world is a multidimensional world where each spiritual plane is as real as the physical. What we perceive as real depends on where we choose to focus. As it turns out, being able to focus my attention, especially in matters of subtle energies, is one of my strengths and it is natural to me.

The unwritten creed of the school is, "Healer, heal thyself." This makes for a most rigorous training on all levels of being, but especially the physical, emotional, and mental relationship with oneself, as the curriculum is designed to help the "new healer" let go of lifetimes of trauma. Well it does work. Honestly, I never cried more than I did in those four years. Some days were so difficult that I wanted to bang my head against the wall and run naked down the street. If it weren't illegal, I would have done so, just to get away from the inner discomfort and trauma that was rising in my body and aura.

Past-life phenomenon was totally new to me. Yet when I started to release these often elusive and painful overlays, there seemed to be no end to them. Pains were rising in my physical body, mysteriously appearing out of nowhere accompanied by strong emotions that would not be contained. A multisensory roller coaster ride cleaned off the barnacles that had attached to my body and field—unfinished (unforgiven) experiences I had collected over lifetimes of trauma that I had been identified with. I learned how to sort through it all, and decided what was mine and what was not. Slowly differentiating and distilling myself, I began to feel who I really am.

I learned to listen deeply with my whole body and being, to myself and to others. I became adept at gathering energy and learning to focus it in a laser-like way to repair the field of another. I refined my ability to feel beyond myself into other realms, to make contact with and enlist support from divine beings who assist us and are available for the asking.

It was here I first encountered the void and thrashed about like a dying fish. Yes, even while going to school and fulfilling my IHD dream, I encountered a momentary void space. In my exhaustion, I finally realized the life-giving, creative darkness of the void and surrendered in peace to what wanted to be. I didn't know I had so much fear in me, lifetimes of it. Fear of alienation, of persecution, and of being alone—it was all in there (in me). But more profound was the realization that it has nothing to do with *who I really am*. I saw that it was not natural to have a nervous system besieged with fear, rooted in old forgotten traumatic memories and running the show of my life. Gradually, I learned to let it all go. I connected to my own inner peace, the beauty and magic of my being, my energetic intelligence, my natural connection to source, and my ability to communicate and cocreate with the divine.

I absorbed the healing knowledge with all my being and integrated what I could immediately in my own self-healing practice. Every night after class, I sat in meditation and figured a way to apply the newly learned healing skills to myself.

Now looking back, I realize that, from day one at BHSS, I developed the Heart Flame Healing program. It was as natural as breathing to me. I initiated sacred space and made contact with my team by way of regular meditation and specific healing requests. I discovered how to track my own body and field by using my pendulum. Advancing my aura and chakra systems, I learned how to affect my own field at will by making regular healing requests and by mastering *the art of receiving*.

Cocreation

In the beginning of my self-healing journey, I noticed that other dimensional beings regularly came to my aid. They made their presence known, letting me know that they were next to me. I could feel the guides at the edge of my aura. They were waiting for permission to enter my field, ready to assist me in my own healing and to upgrade my field. This occurred regularly, especially while in meditation. Suddenly, they appeared at my side. At other times, I would lose interest in a movie that I was watching or a book I was reading, overcome by a momentary need to rest. Reclining, I saw them at the edge of my field—waiting. Then, one of my helpers would move in for another installation to upgrade my field. If the being was female, it would come in from the left of my field, while male helpers would come from the right of my field. They would wait at the edge of my aura, announcing their presence, and move into my field as soon as I gave my permission telepathically to begin the upgrade or restructuring work. This was my clue to recline in order to receive the healing and rest completely.

Many times it was a chakra that needed to be restructured, upgraded, or recalibrated or an organ that needed to be addressed in much the same way. Other times, new energetic lay lines would be laid down through my head, neck, shoulders, and arms and into my hands. In the last eighteen years, I have received thousands of hours of self-healing, upgrades, and changes to my field. This was necessary in order to make it the most efficient and effective template to work with my growing multidimensional support team.

The Hero's Journey and Being on My Own Team

Over time, I fully claimed and refined my own self-healing process. To this day, I practice self-healing with the help of my team regularly, adjusting myself to the highest possibility of well-being and to being able to assist others. The results are immediately tangible and accumulative.

I now enjoy, for the most part, a great sense of well-being, inner peace, and delight in a balanced, creative experience that is my life. That does not mean I am "happy" all the time. Like every other human being, I experience the whole spectrum of feelings and emotions. But I do know how to effectively process, to let go, and to come back to my center and to feeling my essence.

The self-healing journey is most rewarding and absolutely empowering. There is nothing more valuable than knowing that I am the captain of my ship and that I am supported in cocreation with life and the divine. I am delighted to be able to heal myself and others at will and by request. This sacred trinity of myself in relationship with life and the divine has afforded me a life that is better and healthier than anything I could have ever imagined. Actually, this is exactly what I have come to imagine, not just for myself but also for others.

This kind of pioneering high-level healing is, in many ways, uncharted territory. The continuous reworking of the field increases the vibrational frequency of my body, making it more conductive and able to engage with higher levels of consciousness. I did not, however, expect the change that would come about in my organism and how it functions. The ongoing situation with my skin and hands is a function of healing in progress. The gradual but steady expansion of my field has allowed me to reach into pockets of my past that otherwise may not have been excavated. The healing light of consciousness wants to absorb these events now into positive reality.

If there is one thing I know, it is that the healing process takes time and happens in stages. To be an effective guide as a healing presence, I have to know the territory others encounter on their journey. Therefore, I have to be present to all of the details and layers of my own healing process first.

Someone who does not know me and is unaware of the details involved is likely to look at me with worry or pity upon seeing my (often) red, blistered, and swollen hands. They might perceive it as an illness that I am no longer able to tolerate any kind of sugar, as even a single gram of it gives me grief for the duration of two weeks or more. However, I know that my body functions at the highest level. The condition is a means to fulfill the demand for the purest fuel, to master the task at hand with the full availability of my healing presence. As I use my own field and body for my work, my organism is also in service to my purpose and functions according to higher laws. Sugar is now of such low vibrational frequency that it would be like putting sand in the tank of a high-performance car. It is what I had to give up on my hero journey. I herewith *officially* surrender the heroin of the masses, which is sugar!

My diet now consists of oatmeal, eggs, all greens, veggies, nuts (but no cashews), some cheese, and Greek yogurt. Now and then, I can have a dried fig or two or one single piece of dark chocolate. If I stray too far from my diet, my hands will explode into itchy blisters that take weeks to heal. Social events need to be planned for ahead of time by either eating beforehand or taking my own food. Although this may seem like a big ordeal, I have gotten used to it and actually rather enjoy the resulting benefits of eating in this manner. Surprisingly, it turns out that my friends also love my fresh and healthy food. They will often stop by to sample my tasty creations.

What I have learned from all this is that there is wisdom in containment and discernment in service to the greater cause. Sometimes there are habits or things that we must lay down or give up in order to advance and to be truly whole. For me it's been any kind of sugar, flesh, salt, and grains. At this point in my life, I consume only foods that support my cause and leave behind what burdens my body. I have no regrets. I figure it is a relatively small price to pay for the gift of healing and for the honor of cocreating with the divine.

And, yes, I do enjoy myself! On occasion, I will take a calculated risk and indulge in chancy food, as I want to be as others are and enjoy the company of good friends sharing food and drink.

My Team

My team has been growing over time and now includes Kuan Yin, Mother Mary, Jesus Christ, Mother Meera, Hestia, Thor, Buddha, Ganesha, Saint Germain, Bruno Goering, Deepak Chopra, BrooksY, and the archangels, as well as the spiritual surgeons and other deities and beings of the light. They come as needed or invited, and sometimes they will make an extra effort to get my attention in order to be included in my team or to let me know that they are on my team.

Confirmation by Way of Buddha

One early morning while sitting in meditation after a 3:00 a.m. healing session and preparing to go back to sleep, I saw an energy vortex that gathered in front of me in a vertical shape. It was of a most unusual high-vibrational frequency, and I was curious as to who and what was visiting. I asked, "Who are you?"

Immediately, Buddha identified himself with various images of his manifestations. I saw the Golden Buddha, the Chinese Buddha, and the Thai Buddha, as well as the stupas and Buddha heads of Borobudur in Indonesia, which I had visited with Norman many years ago. In an instant, I knew why Buddha had come. For months now, I had heard his name but failed to include him in my healing sessions. Without suggesting any wrongdoing and in the gentlest way, Buddha requested telepathically to be included in my healing sessions.

I was floored and amazed, and I felt humbled and honored all at the same time. I put my hands together in front of my heart and bowed to his majestic presence, giving thanks for his visit. A moment later, I understood that his visit was multifold in purpose. This was year twelve of my healing practice. The Buddha had come to graduate me and give me confirmation of my team. Where church and pastor had failed me so many years ago, I now knew exactly why I was confirmed this time around. Needless to say, the next day, I was walking on clouds.

Lord Ganesha, the Remover of Obstacles

Lord Ganesha is one of the newest members on my team. He showed himself to me for the first time in October two years previous to the time of this writing. I was in Hawaii on the island of Kauai at a seminar when the leader of the seminar took issue with me for one reason or another that I could not understand at the time. I went into deep meditation to get inside the issue and to see what I had done to arouse this contention.

I saw Ganesha. He showed up in his thick-skinned elephant way, taking up my whole inner field of vision until I recognized him and thanked him for coming. Gradually, I got to see that the issue was not personal but a defensive reaction to a past traumatic incident of this young female leader that she herself had not worked out yet.

Since then, Ganesha has shown up regularly in my sessions. It is fun for me to witness my clients seeing and describing him when they encounter him for the first time. A teen female of fourteen years had never even heard of Ganesha and described him as "something elephant," mentioning the thick skin and the long trunk. She said she did not exactly see him but felt his presence.

Jesus Christ

Jesus Christ's presence is most beautiful, physical, and direct. When I was fresh out of Brennan Healing Science School, I was giving a healing session to a dear friend of mine who is a "Jesus freak" by his own admission when the Prince of Peace made his appearance in a very matter-of-fact way. I had been working for about half an hour when a beautiful, exhilarating, and scintillating energy came into my being, filled me up with light, and radiated beyond my physical boundary, extending about an inch beyond my skin. A voice told me telepathically, *I am the Christ*. I knew it to be the truth; there was no doubt about it. It lasted for a few minutes and then subsided, leaving the healing space changed and charged. The Christ had clearly elevated the healing for us both. I didn't mention my experience to my friend until after the healing session. When we compared notes, he told me that he had the most wonderful healing experience while sitting at the feet of Christ.

As it turns out, I'd had a dream weeks before this blessed incident in which I was sitting at the feet of the Christ myself. In the dream, I knew it to be his presence, even though I could only see his feet. It seems I was having a holographic experience of a future that was present at the time of the healing.

Kwan Yin, the Eminence of Feminine Grace

One client on the table witnessed the compassionate presence of Kwan Yin slip gently on a pink cloud from underneath the door and into the healing room. Her presence is most comforting and soft, while she resides regally and humbly in relaxed elegance. As a bodhisattva of compassion, her presence is most healing. She hears the voices of suffering and has vowed to relieve them. She has been with me for many years now, and I don't exactly know when she came to be with me in her most gentle and sweet way.

Mother Mary

Mother Mary is the ultimate symbol of divine love. Her capacity to love is infinite and, to most humans, beyond comprehension. Mother Mary loves to give roses, and often the scent of roses lingers when she is present. I have seen her sweet face descending upon me more than once during deep meditations, and I have called upon her numerous times in healing sessions when my own insight and compassion seemed insufficient. Mother Mary teaches unconditional love, and she has helped me to open my heart in times of need.

Saint Germain

Saint Germain is the master teacher of freedom. I first called upon his presence when I wanted and needed to learn meditation many years ago. His guidance has been most influential in my decision to not let fear rule me or my life but, rather, to make love, freedom, and the fulfillment of my inner heart's dream my prime directive.

Once, while helping a friend's daughter out of the clutches of heroin, as I was working, I felt Saint Germain's blue violet flame come blazing through my own eyes, affirming his presence in the healing and ensuring success. According to Saint Germain, freedom is a choice we make moment by moment in how we focus our attention and by what we choose to believe in, whether we choose love or fear.

Thor

Thor was introduced to me one day when I had questions about indulging in marijuana. I would take an occasional toke of the pipe to enter a more creative space but always had questions about the practice. While I was sitting in a meditation asking my team for help, Thor's mighty presence approached from a distance behind my right side. His heavy footsteps pounded. Weighted down by his enormous hammer, they vibrated the energetic ground he walked on so that I could sense his mighty presence approach my body. I had not ever encountered him before and was quite surprised when he showed up looking so much like an action figure and comic book character. Thor is particularly helpful when you want to let go of outdated habits or addictions.

Mother Meera

Mother Meera is a living avatar, and she resides as of this writing in Germany. I went to see her personally for my own healing many years ago before advancing into my own healer-ship. I found her in a little village in Germany, where she lived at the time. Mother Meera is roughly the same age as I am, and at the time of my visit, I was in my early thirties. An exact protocol dictated the *darshan*, which is the face-to-face blessing with Mother Meera. About 125 people were crammed into a tiny house. Chairs were pushed together with no room in between. We were asked to be silent and move our arms at a minimum.

Mother Meera arrived dressed in a traditional sari. She is East Indian; of small stature; and has long black hair, intensely dark eyes, and a powerful vulnerability that emanates from her being. After her own seating, she spent about ninety seconds with each person. We were instructed to kneel in front of her and put our head in her lap. She worked on the sutures of our skulls. When she removed her hands, we were to sit back onto our heels and lift our heads to meet her gaze.

It took about two and a half hours before it was my turn. Generally, it is difficult for me to spend extended time in close proximity with others, especially when movement is restricted, and this was no different. But I had no idea how the ninety seconds with Mother Meera would immediately change me. When I sat back on my heels to gaze into Mother Meera's eyes, for the first time in my life, I felt that I had actually been seen. With her steady gaze and her Divine Mother presence, she looked into my eyes and down to my soul in the most loving way. I knew that I had been seen, and it was deeply satisfying.

It wasn't until I was back in my chair that I became fully aware of what had happened. I now recognized peace inside of me, and all around me. Looking back, I knew that before the ninety seconds with Mother Meera, I had spent the last two and a half hours in judgment of myself and others. While it was going on, I was unaware of my disturbed state of being. I stayed for another darshan the next day and spent the time in between sleeping in my hotel room. The healing I had received in those ninety seconds with Mother Meera was deep and life changing. The next time I saw her twenty years later, I felt more like her peer.

Deepak Chopra

Many of you may know of Deepak Chopra, the fabulous and famous Indian MD; endocrinologist; and author of countless books on health, healing, and spirituality. I encountered him for the first time in my early thirties. He was giving a lecture on quantum healing, and part of it was a synopsis on how the endocrine system works. I remember sitting in my chair third row back, leaning forward because I did not want to miss a single word of his presentation.

Standing next to the speaker podium, with his right elbow resting against the wood frame and his hands clasped together, he exuded a relaxed confidence that put the whole room at ease and drew the attention of all present. To me, he also had sex appeal. I remember thinking that this man was really fascinating and that I would have really liked to have dinner with him. However, I was too shy to even talk to him when the opportunity arose.

Nevertheless, I was instantly hooked on whatever this man was about—he had it; he embodied it. I received a direct transmission from Deepak, and the information he shared came to me with such ease and grace. My mind and being were flooded with a feeling of wellness as I received knowledge about the natural healing power of our own consciousness. Not once did he look at a piece of paper or a note. His presentation seemed to flow out of him with no effort; it was all knowledge and pleasure. His presence truly inspired me to my core.

I don't claim to have read all of his books, but what I have read inspired me as much as the person. The vast information in his body of work all rings true to me and is scientifically substantiated.

But it was the being itself that made an undeniable impression on me. The balance of knowledge, embodiment, spiritual presence, and the understanding of true wholeness was most inspiring to me. It was so inspiring, in fact, that years later, I requested, via inner channels, to have Deepak on my team. He agreed and instantly became a member of my team. This means that, upon request, I can have conversations with him on the inner planes or in my meditations.

On my most recent birthday, Deepak was the first to wish me happy birthday in the etheric realm. As I sat in my morning meditation, I wondered, *Who is this being with a rather big head congratulating me?* A moment later, I heard his Indian accent and smiled, as I knew it to be Deepak.

Many public figures are available upon request to be on your team. If the purpose of your team is to serve the greater good for all and if it is in general alignment with his or her own world task, perhaps that person who you admire might agree to be on your team. Yes they do have their own lives, but because they serve the greater good of all, often an aspect of their greater being is available for the asking to those like-minded individuals (like myself) who seek support, knowledge, and wisdom for their own world task. Think of them as being on your board of directors, or advisory board. As Deepak is an advocate for spiritual healing and an MD, he is a good match for my team. I love feeling his presence in my sessions and knowing that he is a public person out there supporting my work in general. And of course, I can also reference him through his publications.

BrooksY

My dear friend and mentor BrooksY passed away a little more than a year ago. He, more than anyone, has shown me the possibility and opportunity of my life. By example, he has shown me how to claim myself and my work as the truly unique individual that I am. I owe so much to this beautiful man, who was a personal friend and a mentor to me for twenty-two years. I can say with certainty that I would not be the same person without his input. BrooksY was and is a truly unique being. In his presence, I learned that we are (and that I am) ultimate creative beings. What we say matters! How we relate to ourselves and others creates our reality in detail.

The elegant simplicity of what he taught took years to fully take hold in my consciousness. It was only after he left his body that I truly realized how precious and valuable my time with him was. BrooksY was community oriented and, as such, gathered small groups of unique individuals around him who were his friends and students.

I did not always see eye to eye with my friend and had to leave "the pod" for years at a time to collect myself in other areas. But I would return much to my surprise and find he had yet more vital knowledge to offer, helping me integrate newer aspects of myself and my work.

I can feel and hear my dear friend in my own sessions when talking to my clients; his wisdom, knowledge and uniqueness, blends in with my own in healing conversation. He is the one who has taught me more than anyone about how to choose and live in positive reality and the importance of being gentle with oneself and others. Through BrooksY's presence I came to understand that being gentle is a life skill that we are all lacking and a concept that takes time to fully understand. It is one of his most brilliant elegant and simple gifts he bestowed on me. Thank you for the gift of gentleness that keeps on giving.

Bruno Goering

Bruno Goering was a prominent healer in Germany who suddenly became quite famous in 1949. Below is an internet write-up from the friends of Bruno Goering (www.bruno-goering.org):

Bruno Goering, born in 1906 in Danzig, was a simple workman who moved to Western Germany as a refugee after World War II. Before the war he had various occupations: carpenter, factory and dock laborer, Post Office worker and electrician. Then, suddenly he was the center of public attention. The news of his miraculous healings spread all over the world. From every country came sick people, petitions and proposals. Tens of thousands made the pilgrimage to the places where he worked. A revolution in medicine was impending.

The first time I saw Bruno's photo on the dashboard of friend's car, I immediately felt connected to him. I was not surprised to find out that he was a well-known healer in his time. Instantly I knew him to be on my team, but I only found out in writing this manuscript that he has, in fact, been with me since I was a baby.

Bruno died six weeks before I was born. I understand now that I have been under his protective care and tutelage all along. When he came to me recently upon my request for communication, Bruno told me that his energetic heart beats next to mine and that we are to work more closely together from now on. I felt the truth of that statement even before his telepathic communication in words. His energetic signature is most nurturing and kind.

The Spiritual Surgeons

The spiritual surgeons are a group of other dimensional beings that execute energetic surgeries and medical interventions that are beyond my scope. These beings are likely to have been in physical form and to have served humanity before transitioning, but not all of them have been embodied in physical form. Most of them are task oriented and don't appear warm and fuzzy but rather impersonal.

When a healing is called upon in preparation for a physical surgery, the spiritual surgeons will perform the surgery on the energetic template to support and guide the actual physical surgery.

Bruno Goering is also on my team of spiritual surgeons. Please read "Success and Healing with Spiritual Surgery," the final section in chapter 12, to help you understand more about spiritual surgery.

Part Two

Chapter 7

Why Am I Awake at Three Every Morning?

How we talk to ourselves in those early morning hours determines the quality of our experience for the rest of the day.

—*Karin Inana*

Are you finding yourself awake most nights and at the same time? This is a common occurrence and complaint among many people. They will often say, "I don't sleep through the night; I don't know what is wrong." Perhaps nothing is wrong. Perhaps this is not a deficiency but an opportunity to connect with your very own multidimensional support team. If viewed through the lens of positive reality, being awake during the 3:00 a.m. spot holds a tremendous opportunity for healing and putting yourself in the driver's seat of your life. It might just be your time to be with God or to have a nice chat with your team to strategize your next adventures in life.

Most will agree that it is no fun to toss and turn when others are sleeping (or at least when we assume that others are sleeping). The truth is many of us are awake during the night for one reason or another. I myself had plenty of early-morning restless tossing, watching the clock, frustrated and bothered by my inability to relax and sleep. Then one night, because I was already awake, I remembered how I used to sit in the early morning hours to learn meditation. The next time I was awake at 3:00 a.m., I decided to sit up to meditate, and a whole new world opened before me.

As I sat, I began to appreciate and then to enjoy the early-morning silence. I found pleasure in my own breathing and in hearing my heartbeat. I discovered that it was my time to be with God or source and that having time to be with myself and my thoughts was a gift. It was an excellent opportunity to be with and to communicate with my team and to do my own healing work on myself.

I no longer suffer when I am awake at night, as I know it is my time to be with God. Countless gifts have been bestowed on me in those early-morning hours of sitting in silence. Communication with my team has deepened, as new information and healing skills have been imparted to me, making my life and work more effortless. Those twenty minutes of sitting expand exponentially in my daytime reality. It helps me to be present to the opportunity of the day and everyone I meet. As I have organized myself already in positive reality before the day begins, I am kinder, have more energy, and wear a bigger smile on my face. There is no downside to claiming my 3:00 a.m. spot; it is positive, and I make it my choice. I now love the 3:00 a.m. time so much that I offer distant healing sessions for that time. It's quite a popular spot among my clients, as it is an excellent time to receive healing sessions. This is an example of the win-win situation that can come about in positive reality organization.

So next time you suffer because you are awake at night, see if you want to reframe your reality by deciding to be awake to the opportunity that is presented. But first you would need to let go of the complaint. Rather than even questioning—why can't I sleep?—say, "I accept the opportunity of being awake at this present moment. Thank you for the gift of silence and time." Then sit with a straight spine, perhaps with pillows behind your back for your comfort and enjoy your breath. Observe the ebb and flow of it. Focus your mind on your breath and enjoy the effortless flow of it. If you stay with it, you'll come to find out that life is breathing you! There is nothing you have to do but to enjoy. You might increase your enjoyment by saying out loud or silently (not to wake your bedmate), "I am life. I am life itself. And I am the magic of life. Therefore, life supports me."

See how this feels to you. It is truth; you are life itself. When you state this truth, your organism recognizes this and responds in kind. Try it now. Say out loud, "I am life. I am life itself. And I am the magic of life." Does it not feel really good to you? This statement is grounding and has a tendency to make us feel safer in the world and in our physical body.

How we talk to ourselves in those early-morning hours qualifies how we feel the rest of the night and in our waking time. In doing so, we set the tone to live and act in positive reality for the rest of the day. So make sure you are generous, kind, and gentle with yourself in your early-morning conversation inside the sacred temple of your mind.

I have a dear friend who enjoys gently dancing in the middle of the night when she can't sleep. This is her way of meditating. It has done wonders for her sleep afterward and has increased her creativity and happiness throughout the day. In this way, she is relating to her nighttime waking in positive reality indeed.

What is Positive Reality?

Positive reality has everything to do with our willingness to create a world that is a loving place for everyone, including ourselves, our experiences, and our intended creations. In positive reality, we are inclusive, strive for win-win-win situations, and are free of blame.

Positive reality is based in an experience of joy, compassion, abundance, and generosity. Given the fact that we are ultimately creative beings, what we think and how we act and communicate with each other creates our reality—physically and otherwise. When in positive reality, we entertain positive thoughts about our creation. We are willing to see it through successfully, striving for win-win situations that serve everyone involved in the greater good of all, including our own good. Positive reality is free of fear, blame, or anger and rich in acknowledgement and grateful appreciation.

Fear-based thinking and the resulting actions usually don't make for the best results in our lives down the road. Fear, without the immediate threat to our physical or emotional safety, is mostly a reaction to negative thinking or projection of unhealed past trauma onto the future that is affecting the nervous system in the here and now. The "what if" worst-case scenario is usually based on traumatic experiences of the past or bad news that you have heard that is supported by mass thinking (collective collusion). Decisions based on fear are not likely to be the most creative solution; nor are they likely to be based in the greater good of all.

Positive reality is all about the best or highest opportunity in any situation. It may be that I am awake at 3:00 a.m. unable to sleep, so how I choose to relate to being awake at night will create my waking reality. If I decide that it is a problem and choose to talk about it in that way, then it will become a problem because I promote it as such. I may lament to my friends about insomnia, creating agreement and validation. As a result, I will feel more tired because of it. I might decide to go to the doctor and start taking sleeping pills but will miss the opportunity my team was trying to organize for me in those early-morning hours. Or worse, I might sleep straight through a personal visit from the Buddha.

As an example, the same holds true for the situation with my hands. I may be intolerant to sugar, fruit, meat, fish, fowl, and grain and not able to eat as others do. If I were to see this situation through the lens of negative reality, I might be very unhappy, thinking there is something wrong with me and feeling sorry for myself. But because I know the deeper truth of my condition and I choose positive reality, I have an appreciation for the wisdom and intelligence of my organism. In fact, the intolerance to sugar actually makes my life easier, as I am very motivated to eat only that which supports my health and ability to function at a high level. Sugar is no longer an issue for me. I don't even miss it much, and I love the way I feel without it. At dinners or parties, I enjoy what I can, but I am not tempted by food that will aggravate my situation. Naturally, I don't have to worry about gaining weight, and my clothes will fit for years to come.

Positive reality has everything to do with your willingness to create a world that is a loving place for you, your experience, and your intended creations. The more of your energy centers that are open and fully functioning, the more you will live in joyful, positive, and abundant reality, fulfilling your inner heart's dream.

If you are finding yourself sleepless at night, consider that perhaps members from your team are trying to get your attention by waking you every night at the same time, in order to guide your journey. Have you been asking for assistance or help? It might be that your celestial friends are knocking on your door, standing by, and waiting for your permission and your listening.

Your Team Needs a Way to Find You

Whether you already have a relationship with your multidimensional support team or you are new to the concept and desire to have a team, your team members need a way of finding you. The best way to establish deeper contact is to have regular silent time, preferably in combination with meditation. Meditation helps to clear your mind so that you may be able to hear and decipher the messages that are given. Communication with MDSTs tends to be subtle and often symbolic. I have gotten a lot of information through my dreams or visions in my meditations. But it takes time to establish clear channels of communication.

If you don't have an awareness of your team yet but would like to have one for a specific purpose, go ahead and make a request. If the purpose is for the greater good of all, you have an even better chance of succeeding.

Your Team Is Waiting

Yes, your team members are actually waiting for you to make contact and for you to invite them to help you! Every person has at least one guide. Even right now you have at least one other dimensional being on your team. I say "other dimensional being" because you may have physical people, like members of your family or friends in your life, already in place. In any case, here is a beginning. Start by making a request for communication and/or support. You don't have to know the name of your personal guide to establish contact. I will give an example invocation for you to use as is or modify for your own needs. Make the request in sacred space, and it is sure to be fulfilled.

Ask and you shall receive! In fact, even if you have a guide, you'll still have to make a request for communication to start a conscious relationship. Unrequested interference is a violation of the universal law of free will, so it is not likely to happen. In fact, you might be lamenting a particular problem; however, if you don't actually ask for help, your guide who is aware of your plight and desires to assist, bound by the law of free will, has to wait for the request and the invitation. Remember, a complaint by itself is not a request.

A relationship with your guide or guides is like any other relationship; it needs time and care to develop. If you have a meditation practice, it will be most helpful in your quest to establish tangible communication with your guides and team. But even if you don't have a sitting practice yet, you can start by simply going for a walk and inviting your guide along with you. Make your walk a sacred event to communicate with your guide.

Really, whatever gives you the most joy is a viable way to establish communication and to keep it flowing. If you are a painter or desire to be one, request a guide to that end; it is within the enjoyment of your craft that you'll build and strengthen your relationship with your guide. As you gather your equipment for your chosen focus of your creativity or art, you might request your guide's presence and ask for communication with your muse or guide. It's best if you can make this request out loud. You'll be able to feel the intention of your request as you voice it and receive it by hearing yourself.

The relationship with your team or guides is built on mutuality, availability, communication, and a shared sacred space. Your personal practice is the easiest place to meet up and communicate. A period of dedicated silence is most valuable and supportive of the request. Give yourself the time to settle in without hurry, defense, or angst. Know that you are in caring and supportive company because your divine friends are most attentive, kind, and gentle. But the exchange is much more subtle than in human communication and often given in simple, symbolic ways. So it is best not to have an expectation of a grand message. But do expect an influx of energy that will affect you in a positive way. It may be physical, emotional, mental, and spiritual. It really depends on your personal orientation—of how you perceive life through your personal and unique organization.

Think of your guide as your own high aspiration archived and now advising you. Even though your guides are themselves individual beings, they are now in service by their own free will— to help you bring out what you came here to do. They are here to champion your essence and to make your inner heart's dream manifest, as it lives within the heart of God.

Always feel into your current longing, as it relates to the task and situation at hand. What is your intention? What do you want to have happen here?

Please remember, the information I have shared with you is an accumulation of years of practice. Assembling your team is going to take time and trust in the process. Start slow and go steady. Acknowledge your success; write it down and build on it.

Team Invocation and Invitation

Below is my invocation and invitation to my writing team specifically. This is a sample. Please feel free to change the language to suit your needs.

- You can do this invocation any time of the day and whenever needed or desired.
- Prepare with a short meditation to clear your mind and to make yourself present before you ask to connect with your team.
- Say the invocation out loud.
- Give yourself at least fifteen minutes to be with the experience.
- Contact may be subtle at first, like the feeling of a hand on your shoulder or a change of temperature.
- Do this on a regular basis, and over time, you'll notice the presence of your team distinctively upon request.
- Remember you are cultivating a new relationship. Give yourself plenty of time to practice.
- Don't judge your experience; it will change and refine over time.

Personally I feel more focused and present with my material after I say my invocation. In addition, I ask questions out loud to my team, and they do answer immediately telepathically. Here's an example invocation:

> By the power invested in me, as a fully creative being of God, in multidimensional reality, manifesting in the here and now, I declare this a sacred space for divine contact and communication with my team, muses, and guides for the purpose of writing *Heart Flame Healing*.

> Thank you for your presence, guidance and assistance!

Please help me to put into language the highest truth of what I know so well so that others may have a direct experience and feel the truth of these words.

I turn the writing session over to the Holy Spirit and to the greater good for all.

Thank you; it is done!

Amen

The guides and your team are to be found in positive reality. In other words, neutrality, peace, love, and joy are states of being that allow for an effortless connection with your team or guides.

The words you speak become the house you live in.

—Hafiz

Negative Thinking Can Thwart Your Healing Progress

Fear, anger, and blame are lower vibrational emotional states of being that usually won't allow you to connect to, hear, or sense your guides. The information that comes from an inquiry made in fear, anger, or blame is most likely distorted, as the pathway itself is not grounded in truth. The truth is found outside of blame, anger, and fear in the wide-open space of the unlimited potential of your life and being.

A clarification is needed here about the value of being present with negative emotions without collapsing into them. Of course anger, fear, and blame are in the spectrum of human emotions and need to be felt. But do so responsibly. Don't give yourself over by reacting out of anger, blame, or fear. It will make any situation worse by collapsing your emotional body into the worst possibility imagined. Then, negative emotions will generate your reality.

Rather, be present with your emotion. Feel it and wait until the emotional wave has passed to be able to see and think more clearly. Then decide who you want to be and how you wish to react in this situation.

How do you know you are in a negative state of being? Notice how you are relating with yourself or another. How do you feel or sound to yourself? What is you inner conversation like and how do you talk to yourself? Are you kind, positive, acknowledging, and encouraging? Do you champion yourself? Or is your inner dialogue harsh and tearing yourself (or someone else) down? How you treat yourself is your choice. Just because someone else was less than kind to you does not mean you have to be unkind to yourself. Decide to be your own best friend. Ask yourself, Who would I be if I were my own best friend? How would you talk to yourself? How would you be in relationship with yourself? What would the quality of your inner conversation be like?

Before you make a request, check in with yourself about the state of your being. What is driving you? Hopefully, it is not fear but your longing that is guiding your request.

How Will Your Team and Guides Communicate with You?

How do you wish to receive information and guidance? What is the pathway?

When communicating with other dimensional beings, perceptions are likely to be a more subtle experience, especially in the beginning. Think about the kind of person who you are. Are you more visual, more auditory, or more kinesthetically inclined? And how do you feel about the symbolic language of dreams and synchronicity?

Based on your preference, make a request to your team that the information you are seeking is given to you in a way that you understand or learn best. For example, if you like symbolic dream messages, you may ask for that as one of the avenues of communication. You may also ask to be guided to the right source of reading materials or to be connected to a physically present expert who can help you with your task.

Most of us have the ability to perceive through our senses by hearing, seeing, tasting, smelling, and feeling and also by direct knowing. However, we are all different and uniquely organized beings, meaning some of us are better at hearing, while others have better visual or sensory perceptions. Some individuals are more emotionally inclined to feel into a situation, while others are cerebral and need to think things through. How do you like to learn? Is it by reading and going to class or by direct experience and with a playful attitude?

Practical Tips on How to Connect with Your Guides and Team

Whether you are new to the fun of spiritual transformation and are looking for a beginning or are, perhaps, already adept and wanting to go to the next level in the creation of your life, ask yourself a few questions: What are you seeking to change? Who do you want to be in the world? What experiences do you desire? What kind of a relationship with yourself and others would you enjoy? In other words, feel into your longing as it relates to the different aspects of your life at this moment.

No matter where you are in your life right now, I have a feeling that, if you have read this far, you are most likely up for a new adventure. You might be looking to advance yourself on all fronts. Or you might be feeling stuck or drab. Perhaps you're dealing with an illness or an issue that needs to be resolved. Regardless of the lament, look around in your life and notice where you feel most alive. What is the activity that brings you closer to yourself? When do you feel most like yourself? Or what gives you inspiration?

For me, it is walking, dancing, practicing yoga, and meditation; other times, my work is most energizing to me. I enjoy being with my friends sharing intimate conversation and delicious food. Yet other times, I am drawn to create, enjoying art and beauty.

Find an activity that you can rely on to make you feel better and begin "meeting" with your team on a regular basis. It could be really simple. Perhaps you can have your meetings during your morning walk or on the way back from dropping your kids off at school. Make it an event and actively invite communication with your guides or team by stating it out loud. Make a standing request, meaning, when you get to your daily activity, speak an invocation to invite your team. Repetition and regular practice create and strengthen the energetic pathways, and continuity furthers the relationship over time. New practitioners will take a little time to hone the skill into an art. Allow for the beginner's mind. Know that you are assisted by your team already. It will show in your results.

To this day, I say a healing invocation for myself every time I desire or need a healing. Your sincere request will always be answered; ask and you shall receive. It helps to dispel all doubt! Trust in your honest request! Whether you have immediate proof or not, know that you are being attended to. Notice when your requests are fulfilled and how that fulfillment comes about. Always give thanks and acknowledge when you have received an answer or guidance. It's feedback to your team and solidifies the pathway of your mutual communication. And remember to have fun!

Chapter 8

WHAT IS PAST-LIFE TRAUMA?

*The past is not dead, it is living in us and will be alive
in the future, which we are now helping to make.*

—William Morris

Your multidimensional support team is standing by to assist in all matters of healing and wholeness. Please know you are never alone when resolving past-life trauma. In challenging moments of past-life trauma clearing, these generous light beings come to your side, holding you in love, illuminating what needs to be known, and guiding the way to fulfill your longing in this life. Ask and you shall receive. Your team will come to your side—no doubt.

What is Past-Life Trauma?

Our sacred human heart has specific functions within the aura. One of them is to remember and reconnect us to the wholeness of who we are. It is within the Akashic records of the heart, that we remember who and what we have been in other lives, or past lives.

Severe and/or prolonged trauma in past or present life has a way of leaving scar tissue in the memory of our sacred human heart and the heart chakra. While a person is in the middle of a trauma experience, misconceptions are formed about life in general. Ultimately these misconceptions, as they are born out of trauma, are not in alignment with the truth of life. This trauma experience creates a negative image, or a scar, which is held within the aura, specifically at the level of the heart. The scar tissue is etched into the Akashic memory of the heart, and it remains there until it is activated by a present-life event. Then, the memory bleeds through into the present physical experience, signaling with pain—as the old wound offers itself up for healing. A past-life affliction can be triggered by physical and/or emotional events.

An unresolved traumatic and painful past life (PL) can cause pain in the physical, emotional, and mental body of present-day life. A past-life affliction can come on suddenly out of nowhere, or it can fester and linger as chronic and "mysterious" pain. Unwanted recurring emotions and mental disturbances can also be part of a past-life conglomerate.

A troublesome past life behaves much like unresolved early childhood trauma, affecting the life of the adult. A surfacing past life is often uncomfortable and can be very painful. However, the activation of a PL is always in the direction of healing. Past-life symptoms are often misread and treated as purely physical occurrences. This is because the person suffering or the medical doctor does not know about past-life phenomenon or does not believe in it. Past-life phenomenon is not easily understood. One has to address the issue of reincarnation and other questions when presented with a major PL affliction. Past lives don't care about what we believe; even an atheist who only subscribes to the scientific model can be afflicted.

I have come to understand that we are spiritual beings living in a multidimensional and continuing reality. We move in and out of physical incarnations. One might remember none or a little and others might remember more. A positive past-life experience tends to integrate naturally into our present-day life, gifting us with talents that have been nurtured in other lifetimes.

Past-life experiences are held within the fourth level of the aura on the astral plain. The aura is the living template to our greater reality of who we are as multidimensional spirit beings. When we die, we transition out of the physical realm, but an aspect of the aura continues the journey, including and holding the memory of our sacred human heart. Hence, the aura is more alive then the physical body. At the time of death, the aura completely disconnects from the physical body but retains the memory of the sacred human heart within the fourth level of the field. Levels one, two, and three are dissolved. It is then, at the time of death, when the spiritual animation ceases, that the body begins to decompose. However, the essence of our being continues the journey into unseen aspects of existence.

The Healing Power of Forgiveness

Without forgiveness, there's no future.

—Desmond Tutu

This is a true story on the healing power of forgiveness. In this case, forgiveness resolved bladder and urinary tract issues involving past-life trauma healing. This healing story is my own.

I had been dealing with bladder and urinary tract infections since early adulthood. The first time I recall having a bladder infection was in my twenties. The sudden onset of pain took me by surprise. It escalated in intensity and quickly moved from my bladder to my kidneys, making my back hurt with every movement. I remember going to the emergency room and getting antibiotics, which worked at the time. However, the bladder infections went on to became chronic and problematic. A sensation in my lower belly, which was a painful bladder contraction of sorts, in combination with the sensation of having to urinate all the time, tipped me off to yet another episode. Being on a healing path personally and professionally, I moved away from antibiotics to radionics (energetic medicine), which helped significantly. For the most part, I was relieved to have something that worked. There was, however, an episode—almost ten years ago—that is noteworthy as it demonstrates the healing power of forgiveness like no other personal healing story of mine.

It started with a particularly bad attack of a urinary tract infection. Or so I thought. Experiencing tremendous pain, I could not sit up, lie down, or even stand up. The pain was so extreme that I considered calling an ambulance and going to the emergency room. That being the last resort, I decided to try everything I knew as a healer and listened to my own advice, which is the kind of counsel I would give to my clients.

I felt the pain without defending against it or trying to make it go away. I said to myself, "This pain is information. Allow yourself to get the information that wants to be known." With that, I felt another sensation in my bladder and pelvis. If I really allowed the sensation, it felt like an unwanted penetration.

At this time, I was living with a friend, who also happened to be clairvoyant (clairvoyance is the ability to see beyond the normal realms). I woke him up to help me with this situation. Steven connected with me and looked at my auric field with eyes closed and told me what he saw. A group of young men and boys were standing around, circling a young girl.

The scene was in Africa during missionary times in a past life. I had seen the young African villagers around me in a circle, even before I woke Steven. He then related the whole story to me as he saw it. The little girl was African and had become connected to the missionaries and the gospel they were spreading. She had visions of the mother Mary and was turning away from village traditions, causing a rift in the village. The boys or young men wanted to teach her a lesson and raped her repeatedly, in a tent-like hut away from the village. They ended the foray by kicking her, laughing at her, and mocking her. They asked her, "Where is your mother Mary and the priest now?"

The girl's attackers left her bleeding and half dead, to be discovered by the missionaries. The girl was seriously injured, but she survived. She was cared for and nursed back to health. She lived out the rest of her life on the Mission in service to God, but she was never the same. I saw her clearly in my mind's eye as she was kneeling in prayer next to her bed.

Usually when a past life reveals itself in such detail, the pain associated with that life relinquishes immediately. This particular case was a bigger issue of a time capsule (a past-life event spanning a significant time, with an unresolved conglomerate of physical, emotional, and mental trauma) presenting itself to me. The pain in my pelvis relented. I asked Steven to go back to sleep. I knew I had to resolve this at once, and with this new insight, I had renewed hope. Still feeling intense waves of pain wash over me, I was wondering, What is next? In my mind's eye, I still saw the girl kneeling by the side of her bed in prayer.

Knowing of nothing else to do, I decided to join her at the side of my bed, in my own prayer. As soon as I did, it became clear to me that I had not yet forgiven the young men and boys for the torture and the rape. Given the severity of the heinous acts, it is understandable that one would not ever be ready or willing to forgive, and there are many who would advise against forgiveness in cases like this.

However, this is not how healing works. Forgiveness is essential in healing. To completely heal, to truly erase the trauma of the violence, and to move the experience into positive reality, there has to be forgiveness. Without forgiveness, one is left holding the undesired remains of trauma—including the pain and the weight of a chronic disease—forever. Being a healer, albeit young at the art, I knew this important fact, and I decided to forgive.

Holding back nothing, I forgave the young men out loud right then and there. The effect was an unsurpassed revelation. The pain that had been so relentless upon me lifted in all of five seconds, and within thirty seconds, it was gone completely. I was asleep within minutes, but not before marveling at the true healing power of forgiveness.

I never had another bladder infection. Since then, I have noticed in working with others that bladder and urinary tract issues are often accompanied by remnants of trauma relating to sexual violation in present and past life.

The following is a forgiveness statement that I use with myself or with my clients when a past-life occurrence makes itself known by physical or emotional pain.

Forgiveness Invocation

(Sometimes one has to be willing to just say the words.)

> The invocation reads:
>
> Even though I don't know all of the details of this unexplained pain or sensation I am
> experiencing, it is my choice to forgive it all—
> no matter when it originated, where it originated, or why.
> No matter who was involved or how long it was endured,
> it is my choice to forgive it all, now, completely!
> Including life, God, myself, and anyone who was involved, as well as nature,
> my body, and circumstances, I forgive all
> now completely!
> That is my choice, and thank you!

Be present to the location of the pain sensation as you say it; open up with your consciousness right inside of it. Say the statement and be silent for a few minutes afterward to allow for the release or more information to arise. You might have to say it a few times for different sensations.

Chapter 9

What Is Merging?

Know thyself.

—Socrates

Sometimes the feeling and sensations that you are feeling are not your own; they may belong to another human, or they are bleeding over from a past life that is ready to clear. As human beings, we can and do feel the emotions and physical sensations of others at times. We also have the ability to merge with sensations of pain from our own distant past. Mostly we merge unconsciously without knowing that we have done this and often suffer as a result. Identifying that one has merged is the key to releasing the suffering from one's own body. Merging is a phenomenon that is rarely talked about yet affects most humans on the planet, sometimes positively but, more often than not, negatively. A newborn baby is completely merged with the mother; this natural occurrence in nature and present in animals is also a human necessity and generally accepted as a fact of life. We somehow accept this natural condition of early merging, mostly without translating it into aspects of later life. But a lot is to be gained by recognizing and understanding merging—by bringing into the light of understanding how it can create our personal reality and affect our relationships with others, either positively or negatively.

To fully understand the notion of merging, we have to accept that a shared field or space is alive with consciousness. This means that those who share the common space will qualify the shared space with their presence, thoughts, feelings, and activities. This can be done consciously as in, for example, in a choir meeting, where participants create a harmonious, evolving musical experience. This creation is usually enjoyed by all and is for the greater good of everyone, including those who come to listen. It is fair to say that anyone who comes into the practice session of the choir might have a shift in mood and will be elevated or at least changed to some degree. If the choir practice is good, one's heart may open upon entering. Hearing mellifluous heartfelt voices honoring and praising God, life itself, or the angels, might lift your mood. A grievance in your heart or a grudge holding another in contempt might be dissolved in the merging with the common intent held and expressed by the choir in the room. It might very well be a lasting effect, returning peace of mind to the one who came to listen. Even after leaving choir practice, one feels lighter, and there seems to be more space to the heart. This is an example of positive merging. It's the kind of merging we agree to by entering into an experience like a movie or a performance. We expect to be impacted, made to feel something, or to be inspired.

When we decide to go to a three-hanky movie, we know beforehand that we will most likely cry. We choose to merge with the story told; with the intention of the author, director, and actors; as well as with the musical score, which is designed to drive home the point. By agreement and design, it all becomes one. And if a movie is really good, it's like magic. Then, we are transported, even transformed, elated, and relieved; we are perhaps imbued with hope for our own lives by a happy ending. Or we find ourselves musing over a serious drama, connecting to the database of our common human soul body; we search for a place where we can find more understanding to better relate.

But the kind of merging I am addressing here is emotional and unconscious merging, where one is absorbed into an unwanted experience of emotional intensity and loses oneself to it. This is unconscious merging with emotions generated by others that, thus, affects your own being. It may be an experience of being overcome with anxiety, fear, hopelessness, anger, or depression, often seemingly out of nowhere. The "other" might be a spouse, a family member, or a friend. But negative unconscious merging can also occur with peers, classmates, fellow company employees, people who you watch on the news, and all other global inhabitants.

Energetic emotional merging is quite a big subject, and it's not much talked about, partly because not many people really know about it. But talk to a sensitive like me, and you'll get plenty of head nods to signal understanding of the challenge presented. Merging can take your peace of mind and render you defenseless against fear of survival and the depression of the masses, meaning other humans. If you don't know how to differentiate and feel yourself as "who you are in your own emotional autonomy," you might easily be absorbed into another's emotional riptide. You may not know how you came to be out on the choppy waves of the ocean being tossed about by waves that are way above your head. As you search for a reason in the theater of your own life, it seems to take you out even further into the now dangerous currents of the open sea. As big waves of anxiety hit your emotional body, you fear drowning. Then anxiously treading water to save your life, you hope your feet will soon again find safety on solid ground. Or if you are feeling really hopeless, you might thrash about. You may, in turn, exhaust yourself and others by clinging too much. The cycle of negative unconscious merging may continue to take its toll on your family and friends. And in the end, nobody wins; everybody feels taken down a few notches.

Does this sound like a familiar state to you? Such was Teresa's state when she found me; she was anxiety ridden for no good reason. In other words, one explanation for it was as good as the next. Psychological counseling had brought little or no relief but had made her feel agitated and burdened. Because she could not figure out what the matter was, she feared that she had a more serious affliction.

Teresa is a lovely feminine Latina woman in her early thirties. She is small of stature, has a delicate frame, is sensitive, and is an empath. She came to me because she suffered from unreasonable fear and anxiety. We worked together for a few years off and on as needed. She received the full recalibration of her aura and her chakra system by way of restructuring, past-life trauma clearing, and spiritual surgery. Teresa's body relaxed as her physical and energetic body got grounded. She also felt more secure in her the rest of her life and enjoyed a previously unknown calmness in her body and being. Physically, she filled out and took on a more womanly shape, which took her some getting used to, as the frame she was accustomed to was that of a girl. She became more confident, expressive, took charge of her life, and adopted a more adventurous attitude.

After finishing her graduate work as family child therapist, Teresa decided to work abroad in the Dominican Republic for the duration of a year. She wanted a different perspective, to live in another culture, and to use the experience to advance her career. While Teresa was in the DR, we occasionally worked together as needed over distance, while communicating by email and texts.

During her stay in the DR, Teresa got robbed three times. This violent and unfortunate experience made her feel physically and emotionally unsafe. But it also brought up issues of trust, affecting her relationship with her new boyfriend, to the point where she would question his character.

While Teresa lived and worked in the DR, old patterns of anxiety returned. Feeling insecure, she questioned her newfound relationship and doubted herself again. After a few distressed emails, it became clear to me that Teresa had been affected by the robberies and had also energetically merged with the general survival issues present in the DR. These included poverty and a general lack of resources—issues that make one feel less safe in the world and will distort the first chakra. Living under these kinds of circumstances will then be a fear-based experience. All of this was undermining Teresa's best efforts to stay grounded, as she was merging with the emotions and mind-sets of those around her. It occurred to me that Teresa would never feel completely safe in the poverty-stricken DR and that perhaps her journey in the DR was complete. I asked her if it was time to come home Teresa agreed with my assessment and made arrangements to return home with her newfound love back to the United States.

Here are some excerpts from the emails Teresa and I exchanged after the aforementioned healing session:

> Teresa,
>
> Your field seems to go down by way of merging with your surroundings. There are general survival issues where you are in the Dominican Republic. This is affecting and undermining the state of your field. It is the reason I am advising you to make a move back to the States. I think you got what you went for. What do you think?
>
> K
>
> Thank you so much for the insight, Karin. I completely agree with you. And by coming here, I have learned so much about myself, specifically my environment and surroundings ... And now more than ever, I have really understood that about myself—that I need to be in a nurturing, safe-feeling, positive, environment ... And I think it will help me in the future when I decide to buy a home somewhere, wherever that may be. Thanks again, T

This story is a classic example of how negative merging can sneak up on you. Teresa is a sensitive who picks up on the state of other human beings, intentions, and the level of consciousness in the human energy field—the space that is shared by all. Her finely tuned nervous system records and responds to the existential fears of others. By way of merging, she gets to experience and know the energetic lay of the land, as well as the underlying intent. Unfortunately, she also loses herself a little, as she is still learning how to differentiate herself, which is a healing skill on its own. That was why she continued to reach out to me. As I said earlier, merging is a big issue for a sensitive, empathic person like Teresa. It takes time to understand the concept and to get a handle on what is actually happening in energetic reality.

If first chakra issues were a problem to begin with, a prolonged threatening situation will test the durability of progress already made. It may appear that one is going backward, as old patterns seem to reemerge. But what happened here is that Teresa received and responded to the wake-up call. Her newly grounded nervous system actually knows what it feels like to be safe and secure. Hence, she was deeply perplexed about feeling ungrounded and insecure, prompting her to a deeper investigation. Her field had not failed her but actually served her well. By becoming aware that she was merging with negative mass consciousness, she was able to differentiate herself and acknowledge, "This is not truly me. This feeling of unease is generated by the poverty and general survival issues in the DR." And with that, she made her decision to leave.

Merging with another can be experienced as a physical sensation, meaning the pain in your back or hips may not be your own. One night, I shared with my friend Tulla what I was writing about, and she said to me, "Make sure that you write about the incident of my hips." The incident she was referring to had occurred about five month previous to our conversation. She then went on to remind me in detail what had happened to her.

Tulla is exotic-looking. She's a five-foot-ten, dark-haired, olive-skinned former fashion model whose image used to grace the cover of *Vogue* on a regular basis. Tulla now expresses herself as a musician and artiste. She is very passionate and a fun human being to be around. I enjoy her company immensely. It was pre-Christmas season party time last year. She had come over to have dinner with me and to catch up. Tulla chatted away about a party she had been to the night before, how she had connected with the host of the party in a rather profound way, and that he felt like an old friend to her. Excitedly, she showed me a photo of them together that had been taken on her phone the night before. I recognized the face, as I had seen the man in the photo in quite a few movies. He was a seasoned actor with a long prolific career as a lead character actor. The photo showed them both smiling, and there was warmth between Tulla and Emo. As they were leaning into each other, I could see and feel the connection. These were old friends happy to be reconnecting and enjoying this special moment together.

Then my beautiful friend went on to a different subject, lamenting pain and stiffness in her hips that had appeared overnight it seemed. With a painfully twisted face, Tulla told me that she felt like an old, crusty person, fearing arthritis might have invaded her hips. She had woken up that morning barely able to move or walk. With a puzzled look on her face, she asked me, "Can arthritis come on overnight?"

I took a step back and, for a moment, just observed. I listened to her as she went on about her hips, pointing to them and expressing how painful the experience was. I understood her concern and felt her distress. It came to me suddenly. In a flash I recognized that she had merged with her newfound old friend. She was feeling "his pain" in her hips.

Sharing my thoughts with Tulla, I explained to her that the profound connection between her and her friend had opened the door to merging, by way of their shared heart connection.

I gave her a "healing command" to speak right away. Here is the command: "It is my choice to feel myself as who and what I am only!" And then add firmly, "*Right now!*"

Tulla spoke the command and, a moment later, looked at me in surprise. Her mouth gaping like she was in shock, she pointed to her hips. "Oh my god. It is gone. I can't believe it's gone!" Then with a big smile on her face, she added, "I have my hips back." She did a little happy dance.

But she kept checking her hips all evening to see if the change would last. And yes, for the most part, it did. As it turns out my friend was feeling Emo's pain but was able to immediately differentiate herself with the simple statement I gave her.

Merging with Your Own Trauma

A week later, I got a bewildered call from Tulla. She was calling to tell me that the pain in her hips had returned, yet to a much lesser degree. Looking into the matter by focusing with my third eye on her astral body, I saw that Tulla had merged with her own past-life trauma. When I related this to her, she immediately saw herself as an old woman, disfigured by arthritis, bent over in obvious pain, and moving about in a slow and decrepit way.

I asked Tulla to repeat the command I had already shared with her. "It is my choice to feel myself as who and what I am only. Right now!"

As soon as she spoke the command out loud, the pain in her hip moved out of her body. Tulla had to do this a few more times to fully release the past-life trauma from her field, until the entire residue disappeared from her body.

What happened is that Tulla's contact and merging with her friend Emo had activated her own past-life trauma to such a degree that it came up in her own consciousness and body to be released. This is all good news when one knows about merging and can view it through the lens of healing in positive reality.

However, if this happens to an uninitiated person, he or she might go into reaction to the painful physical manifestation of merging and claim it as his or her own. Now the person, carrying both his or her own and the other's trauma, might be in for prolonged suffering as a result of an otherwise positive meeting with a dear old friend. I know that sounds quite messy, but it happens quite often. This is usually the point where the afflicted seeks out medical advice and undergoes a series of tests and scans. These often reveal inconclusive results, prompting a diagnosis of psychosomatic trauma—meaning it's all in your head.

From my perspective, it's all in the heart, or the astral body.

Past-life memory is stored in the layer of the aura that governs the emotional and spiritual heart. Past-life memory is stored in the fourth level of the field of the aura, which is also called the astral body.

I think it's important to mention that I fully support a full medical investigation of symptoms to cover your basis. However, most doctors and medically trained professionals have very little or no knowledge of past-life trauma and how it can affect the physical body. For that reason, they will only suggest medical treatment for the issue in question.

The sections that follow recount personal examples of merging.

A Comedy of Merging

Not long before writing *Heart Flame Healing*, I took a weeklong performance workshop in a progressive educational retreat center, about six hours up the coast from here. It was my once-a-year getaway opportunity to mingle with like-minded individuals and to expand my horizon by experiencing other types of healing modalities.

At the end of the workshop, all participants were asked to gather for a completion meeting and a last feedback from our coach, Rita. The feeling in the room was one of excitement, glee, and satisfaction, as the workshop had been a smashing success according to staff and our group of about twenty attendees. I ended up sitting next to Luke, a lanky, self-effacing, Bukowski-esque writer and recovering alcoholic from Australia. He had been clean and sober for a few years at that point. Sitting next to him, I felt a level of tension passing between us, not the grounded alert relaxation that I was used to but a shifty uneasiness.

One by one, everyone in the group went up on stage. We said our goodbyes with a last remark and an address to the room. As Luke was up on stage, I noticed his third eye was very dark and clogged—a combination, perhaps, of years of drinking and negative thinking. I also saw the effects of other drugs in his field and what looked to me like a steady consumption of marijuana. I held no judgment in regard to the matter but was surprised to see the effects of the drugs in Luke's field. It was so clear that it struck me, and I took note of it.

After Luke sat down, again next to me, I again became present to the discomfort between us. Crossing his legs away from me, his arms folded in front of his chest, and the hand closest to me propped up and shielding his face, Luke displayed a body language that clearly discouraged contact between us. I tried to make my field soft to harmonize with him, which helped a little. Despite my effort to stay neutral, soon, discomfort took over once more, making both of us, but especially him, quite squirmy in his seat. Much to my surprise (because I don't smoke), I had the thought, "I can't wait to get out of here and have a smoke." Then, a scratchy feeling irritating my throat was threatening a cough that I desperately tried to suppress.

Unable to concentrate, I sat there clearing my throat and heaving, until finally I broke out coughing uncontrollably. As it was disturbing to the ongoing process in the room, I got up and out of Luke's field for the coughing to subside. Standing behind my chair, I knew that I had just merged with Luke's desire to smoke and felt that he knew it too. Naturally, after I sat down again next to him, there was more squirming from both of us. Luke did not want to be sitting next to a sensitive who could feel his intent, and I did not want to be crowding his space with my sensitivities either. There was only one thing to do—choose to be comfortable in an uncomfortable and comical situation.

Relieved at the conclusion of the workshop, I bolted for the door as soon as it was over and only said the most necessary goodbyes to a few of my classmates on my way out. As much as I had enjoyed the experience, it had been an intense week of togetherness, and I needed some space to reorganize myself and to digest the events of the week.

While in my car traveling to my next destination, I reviewed the event and the situation with Luke. Merging with Luke had taken place in the lower three layers of the aura, physically emotionally, and mentally. In layer three, which is mental, I had picked up his thoughts. In layer two, I had experienced his emotional agitation. And in layer one, which is part of the aura relating to the physical body, I had felt the strong urge to smoke.

For me, this was by far the clearest and most distinct experience of merging with another. I was present to it as it unfolded and not after the fact and, therefore, able to differentiate myself in the moment. As Luke was on stage, I saw that his third eye was clogged, clouding his perception. By not accepting his negative state of mind as my own, I was able to let go of any judgment concerning Luke or myself. This allowed me to return to my happy equilibrium and keep the wisdom and value of the teaching moment in this comedy of merging.

Emotional Merging with a Group

In June 2004, a few days after Ronald Reagan had passed, while on my way to my office, en-route from Ojai to Santa Monica, I had a surprising experience. Halfway through my hour and a half long drive, going along Las Posas Road through a green belt that passes right by a small airport, I encountered a congregation of people. I thought it was strange to see a group of about thirty or forty people standing on the side of the road where usually only farmworkers tooled about.

As I approached the group, I could also see a plane in the distance, just about to take off. The plane was a commercial plane and considerably larger than the usual two- or four-seat passenger planes that I had seen taking off from this airport. A moment later, as I was driving through the group of bystanders on the side of the road, I was overcome by intense emotions. Within seconds, a deep feeling of loss, grief, and sadness for the former president of the United States came over me. I was completely taken over and surprised by the projectile tears coming out of my eyes, streaming down my face. In that moment, I knew the plane was to fly the former president's body back to Washington for the state funeral. All of this happened within less than a minute, as much time as it took for me to drive through the grieving congregation.

Exiting the emotional conglomerate of the group, my tears stopped immediately, and I was back to feeling my neutral self. Wow, what intense emotion right out of the blue. Completely taken over, I was unable to edit my reaction to it; the group merging in communal grief was so strong that it had swept me up in its tide.

As you can see, there are many ways of merging. And in a way, if one doesn't get stuck in it, it is just information. But if one doesn't know that one has merged with an experience generated by others and claims it as one's own, it can be a confusing situation at best and uncomfortable to excruciating if you have merged with the physical symptoms of another (as in Tulla's story). If you ever question whether what you are feeling and experiencing is your own, ask yourself, *Does this experience feel like me?* Of course you would have to have a pretty good idea of what "you" feel like, in order to differentiate yourself from merging with another person or experience.

How to Unmerge

The best way to unmerge is first and foremost to know what you feel like as the unique individual who you are physically, emotionally, and mentally. Exercise is tremendously helpful short and long term, as it gets you back into your own body and helps you to differentiate. Any kind of exercise works better if you really enjoy it. For that matter, any activity that you truly enjoy will help you get back into the experience of who you are.

Beyond that, it helps to connect with one's core essence. Meditation is most beneficial in cultivating and becoming familiar with your own energetic signature, or core essence.

If you think you may be merging with someone else's trauma, find out if this is the case by first saying, "I allow it!" Then be present and ask yourself, *Does this experience really feel like me?* If the answer is no, say the following statement out loud: "I allow all that which is not me to pass through me without residue, and I pass it on with a blessing of ease and grace—now!"

Follow up with, "I feel myself as who and what I am—only!"

Whenever you can, say these statements out loud and give it a few minutes of your undivided attention. In other words, be present to what is and really do *allow it*. Meet the experience with curiosity and compassion. If it does not feel like you, most likely it is not you, and you are merging. Knowing that it is not you makes unmerging easier. Judging the experience, yourself, or the other tends to prolong merging.

It is important to note again that merging is natural. If you choose to live in positive reality, it is just information. You are reading the energetic information of the shared common field. There is no need to judge or to defend against it. "I allow it" is a good statement to begin with. It will remove the defensive stance and fear factor, as you will be willing to be present with what is. Go through all of the above mentioned statements, give it about five minutes, and then decide what else needs to take place. Perhaps it's a meditation, a walk, a dance, or a visit to the gym. Talking it over with a friend can also be helpful. But it is important to not judge the experience or vilify the person you may be merging with.

Chapter 10

THE IMPORTANCE OF MEDITATION

*Meditation makes the entire nervous system
go into a field of coherence.*

—Deepak Chopra

When you pray, you are talking to God, source, or the universe; when you are meditating, you are listening to the source of all. The practice can tune your inner ears to the highest opportunity of the present moment at any time or in any situation. When you are tuned in, you can easily feel where your blessings reside and choose that which resonates with your highest good.

The best way to differentiate, to unmerge yourself, and to get to know yourself as *who you are* is to sit in meditation. As a daily practice, there is nothing more powerful that you can do for a healthy thriving mind and body. Meditation takes a prime position right alongside diet and exercise in changing your life for the better. No matter where you start out, I invite you to see the purpose of meditation in service of your best life. It will help you to align with what is being presented, in the highest possibility and for your greater good.

Meditation will help you become familiar with the feeling of your own essence, while clearing outdated belief systems and habitual negative emotions as they are felt in the body and mind.

The practice of sitting gives time and location for your team to find you—to guide you in matters close to your heart. No matter what kind of meditation you choose to practice, it is likely to return 1,000 percent for your investment.

Meditation is one of the best ways to begin to differentiate yourself—to know yourself as the unique individual you are. It helps you become conscious and present to what you really feel like on the inside, which at the depth of your being is your core essence. There is probably nothing that feels better than experiencing and enjoying your core essence. Other names for core essence are divine essence or the core star, which is akin to the Holy Grail that we are hoping to find when embarking on a vision quest or soul-searching journey.

We all want to know that we matter and that we have light and a purpose. Even though many of us pray that, at the core of our being, we will find something real—a spark and a light that shines with true goodness that is unique to our own being—there may be a fear attached to this longing. Leftover traumas from the past generate negative emotions and thoughts that are less than kind to the sacred self and seek to tear it down. Secretly, we fear that what we will find is dark and dirty, like the thoughts and emotions that are ruining our best efforts to have a good time with family or friends on a perfect Sunday afternoon. And hence, one might avoid the sitting cushion, mentally labeling it a trapdoor to stay clear of and procrastinating the enjoyment of his or her true inner light.

But fear not, these are mostly mental and emotional habits that don't serve you any more, presenting you with the very reason to sit down to clear them out, for good! You may have become so familiar with the mental/emotional inner tension and anxiety that you have mistakenly identified with them as part of your own character.

Here is another thought on the matter of mental disturbances; it is possible that not all those frustrating thoughts and emotions you experience are your own. As described in the previous chapter, you may have merged with another in your circle, picked up his or her "negative" mental chatter, and are now riding on the emotional cloud of another. Unable to identify the origin of distress, you have claimed it as your own and are now struggling to it let go. Trying to process this kind of debris only adds to the dilemma and tends to make it worse.

At the end of this chapter, I will share with you a simple meditation that is easy to practice and powerful in and of itself. But if you need more guidance, I encourage you to seek out what you need to be able to have a meditation experience that you'll enjoy. There are many ways to meditate and no shortage of books, recordings, and now even downloadable apps available on the subject. The wide-reaching benefits of meditation have been researched and are scientifically substantiated. And while it is certainly good to inform yourself and to read up on the subject, it is my hope that you will dive right in, because, as soon as you start, the benefits will flow. Practicing makes learning easier too.

According to research and personal experience, here are just a few things that are likely to happen—lessening of and eventual freedom from anxiety, peace of mind, a greater ability to focus, improved quality of sleep, and a general feeling of happiness. At a recent visit to my prosthodontist, I had a conversation with my doctor about the benefits of meditation, as he had taken up the practice of late. He said he no longer worries about the small stuff that used to bother him and now enjoys more peace of mind. With a bright smile, he continued, telling me that his wife is much happier as well. So if you need yet another reason to take up meditation, do it for the one you love; it might just improve your relationship.

Personally, I can't visualize my life without my sitting practice— just as I can't imagine my life without brushing my teeth. If I don't, I know my teeth are likely to deteriorate and eventually fall out. Here is a little visualization for you; mentally project the consequences of never brushing your teeth again into your future. Voila! The truth of that reality is something nobody wants to think about, so we all brush—morning and night! Now imagine what a regular sitting practice could do for you and mentally project your creative light out into your future. I trust this vision is encouraging and brings a smile to your face.

Sitting is a simple meditation:

> Sit in a comfortable position with your back straight and your eyes closed. Your feet are either on the ground or folded underneath you. Your eyes are closed and resting behind closed lids. Observe your breath and let your thoughts flow by. Keep your focus on your breath and notice what floats by the screen of your mind. Don't engage. Observe. Let the thoughts go by! Keep coming back to enjoying your breath.

Sitting clears out my mind of all the things that want to poke holes into my peaceful being. Sitting is the first and last thing that I do on most days. And I have been practicing for the last twenty-five years. In the morning before I get out of bed, it helps me organize myself to the highest opportunity of the day ahead and again at night to let go of anything that I might have picked up during the day. After my sitting or meditation practice I also make adjustments to my field and often receive healing from my team, aiding a better night of sleep. The time investment of five, ten, or twenty minutes is guaranteed to return a multitude of dividends.

For the purpose of this book, which is to discover and realize your heart's longing, meditation is key, as it will help you connect to your greatest truth in any moment or situation. Additionally, meditation will solidify your connection to your multidimensional support team, as it will enable your team members to find you in a heightened receptive state while on your sitting cushion, making conscious communication with your team possible.

Your sitting practice will help you to let go of all that you are *not*. Over time, the practice distills your essence, enabling you to know and enjoy who you really are. As effortless creativity flows easily from the baseline of your pure essence in alignment with your purpose, get ready for your life to shift into high gear.

Meditation Is Medicine for the Success of My/Your Life

My preferred style of meditation is called Vipassana meditation. Vipassana means to see things as they really are. It is a meditation of self-observation; you sit in silence and observe physical sensation, emotional landscapes, feelings, and mental thought patterns.

Insisting on "total" silence of the mind is futile and will likely be frustrating to your best efforts, as even the most experienced meditator will have some thoughts during a sitting. The trick is not to jump on the train of your thoughts and run away with it but to observe your thoughts with some detachment and without judgment. Especially in the beginning of your meditation or sitting practice, it will be helpful to have something to focus on to prevent the monkey mind from running the show. Focusing your mind on observing your breath is an easy method that any beginner can do. No matter what happens—if your mind wanders, if you have an itch, if you're distracted by noise or by the delicious smell of coffee wafting in from the kitchen—simply return your focus to the physical feeling of your breath. Know that you are life and that life is breathing you. Become a witness and observe the natural movement in your midsection, generated by your breath. If you stay with it long enough, you are likely to feel and even hear your heart beat, and that, in turn, is your passageway to the mystical chambers of your sacred human heart. So much can be explored from here as you tune into your heart, it will communicate with your conscious mind and surely reveal *the heart of the matter.*

Sit with a straight back with either your feet on the ground or cross-legged underneath you; this is the recommended physical posture. A chair or a couch with pillows behind your back works well, as does the headboard of a bed to support your back. Regular sit-ups and a yoga practice are known to build a strong core and will prevent you from collapsing forward during your meditation.

In the beginning, some parts of your body can become rather loud and uncomfortable during your sitting practice; your legs may fall asleep, or your back may spasm. Again—allow, observe, and return to your breath. It is your body's way of letting you know where it needs strengthening or stretching. Take note, heed the call, and make the choice to give your body what it needs. Including your body's needs in your meditation project can elevate your practice to the art of self-healing and eventually facilitate a harmonious body-mind connection.

Over time and with diligent practice, meditation will secure a harmonious connection not only with your body-mind but also with your higher soul consciousness. From there, it will help you establish a lasting and beneficial connection with your multidimensional support team. This creative triad of body, mind, and spirit grants you access to command your own bioenergetic computer. This means that you'll be able to make adjustments to your aura at will. Your skillful practice then becomes an art that you'll love to revisit on a daily basis, as it returns your birthright, which is the most valuable gift—the power to heal yourself!

A Simple Breathing Meditation

- Choose a place that you will be comfortable sitting for ten minutes; it may be a chair, your sofa, or your bed.
- Sit with a straight back. It may help to have your feet on the ground.
- Set your timer and make sure that you are undisturbed; turn your phone on silent.
- Close your eyes and focus on the natural ebb and flow of your breath for ten minutes.
- If your mind wanders, keep coming back to your breath.
- Be kind to yourself. Do not to judge your thoughts. Just notice them and come back to your breath.
- Be present to the sensations of your body, like your chest rising and falling with each breath, and allow them to be.

The above meditation is simple but powerful if practiced

regularly. The idea is to clear out the busybody mind and to become more present to the feeling of who you really are. That means allowing thoughts to be if they arise. Don't judge them; let them go by and keep on focusing on your breath. Feel the movement of your chest rising and falling with your breath. Get into the rhythm of it and enjoy! Notice how you feel afterward. You might want to keep a journal to keep track of your progress.

Chapter 11

MAKING SPACE FOR YOUR NEW LIFE

*Abundance is a process of letting go; that
which is empty can receive.*

—Byrant H. McGill

Meditation will help to clear the mind. But when you open your eyes to see clutter crowding your life, it might be time to clear out the old, worn out, and unused to make space for your new life.

So, my dear friend, are you ready and longing for your new life but experiencing more of the same old, same old? It could be that there is too much "same old" in your life, holding outdated patterns in place. Look around your house, at your desk, closet, and refrigerator. Does it reflect back to you and inspire your new life? Or is the same old science project hiding in the back of your fridge, making you reach for the phone to order Chinese food or a pizza—only to realize at the last bite that it wasn't all that good and what you really wanted was a healthy home-cooked meal?

How about your closet? How do you feel when you open it, looking for the ensemble to fit the occasion of the day? Are you frustrated while sorting through a jumbled mess of clothes that are not inspiring? Do you finally settle on an outfit that does little for your self-esteem but is all that you could find that fits or is clean?

How about your living room? Does it invite and inspire your new life? Do you have enough space in your living room to dance if the tango is tugging at your limbs? Or are too many possessions in need of management and crowding the freedom of your self-expression? Whether it's the tango, yoga, or painting, no matter what the focus of your inner heart's dream, it has a much better chance of thriving if you give it a space in your life. That means an actual place—a domain in your house that is assigned solely for that practice or interest.

Where do you practice your craft, meditate, write, dance, or practice yoga? Look around in your space. What do you see? What do you feel? Who lives here? Have you claimed yourself as *who you are* in the space where you live? What needs to change?

Every year, I make it a point to move into my living space again, to clear out and renew. Sorting through all my possessions, I let go of what no longer supports my best and highest life. These days, I start with my fridge, as the quality of my life and what is in my refrigerator are intimately connected. Not too long ago, I opened my refrigerator and found no inspiration, instead feeling repulsed by the old containers in the back. They had been there for quite a while, and I dreaded dealing with them. But wanting a fresh start and a sparkling clean refrigerator, I made the commitment to clear out my fridge right then and there. It took a few hours to take out all of the things, sort through it all, and throw most of it away. Then came the task of cleaning the fridge. Gradually, the initial annoyance over the duty of it gave way to the good feeling of getting it done.

Cleaning out the fridge also cleared out some leftover desires for foods that are no longer working for me. At this time, it had been over two years since my body decided to give up wine, sugar, salt, meat, and fish, as well as basically all processed foods. But I kept the cheese. Yay! Gone into the trash are the truffle chocolate, the wine, and the energy bar made out of organic beef that beckoned me at Whole Foods six month ago but was hiding nine grams of sugar, as well as an olive condiment with too much salt.

As I cleaned out the fridge, I committed to only stock that which is good for me. My body thrives on vegetables, greens, whole milk yogurt, and nuts. I know that, if I provide my organism with what it truly needs, the rest of my life flourishes right along with it. Afterward, while proudly stocking my clean fridge with all that is good for me, I discovered a new way of combining my food. It was there before, same ingredients, but now I saw it! Peas, avocado, and gnocchi with Asiago cheese, a touch of pickled lemon, pine nuts, and butter—yummy! It has become one of my favorite dinner choices (and only takes ten minutes to make). The point of the story is that letting go of what does not serve me anymore makes room for a new wave of creativity.

Next stop is the closet—to let go of old clothes, to gift away some items, and to recreate. Clearing out the closet of outdated garments can be a liberating and creative experience. Shedding your old skin reveals the new and gives way to discovering the unique style of your life. This is an easy and fun task for me. I enjoy clearing out and giving away the threads that have not seen the light of day in two years, including those items that no longer express my best and highest self. The rest goes into the recycling bin. But if you dread your closet clean out because you don't know what to let go of or keep, you might benefit from the help of a friend or even a professional stylist. One of the best investments I ever made was the good money I spent on a professional stylist.

Our garments function as our second skin and signal to others who we are and what we are up to in the world. As such, our clothes deserve our careful consideration. Ask yourself, *Does my wardrobe express the unique individual that I am?*

How do you feel in what you wear? Be willing to let go of garments that don't express who you are right now, as well as those that have been on the hanger unworn for two years or more. Make space, have fun, and accept the good fortune of your new life. Chances are, the more room you make, the better you will feel.

How about your desk? As you walk up to your desk, are you inspired to move ahead on your projects? Is it organized to conduct the business of your life with efficiency and ease? Does it represent your longing in some way? Or do you sigh at the sight of the mess piled up on your desk and make a U-turn for the sofa, because looking for that contact or paper seems too much of a big deal? Besides being the place where you are most likely to pay your bills and connect to the rest of the world, in your home or office, your desk also symbolizes your authority and success.

Now how about your bedroom? Is the place where you dream and sleep comfortable nurturing, clean, and clear in energy? Or are you haunted by ghosts of the past, unable to rest deeply enough to dream and recharge? Do you wake up already agitated and present to fear?

If the latter is true, you might want to start with your bedroom. There you can clean and clear out all that is not needed, used, or enjoyed. If a major crisis like illness, loss, or divorce has kept you up at night, chances are you might benefit from a salting of your mattress. Yes, you read that right. Salting your mattress will clean your nest of the emotional and mental trapdoors that were left on your mattress in times of extreme stress. Reoccurring thoughts and emotions create a swamp, a conglomerate and consciousness that, if negative, will contaminate your bed. Thus, every time you bed down to sleep, that established pattern of stress or illness will inform your consciousness. Even if this energetic contamination is subtle to most, it will still be felt.

To salt your bed, get a pound or two of rock salt or Epsom salt. Strip your bed down to the mattress and evenly pour the salt over it. Spread it out to make sure the whole mattress is covered. Let it sit for twelve hours and then remove the salt by scooping it up and vacuuming the rest. Redress your bed with clean sheets and get in to feel the difference. Happy dreaming to you!

If you are still unsure where to start, choose the area in your home you most resist and want to avoid. That will be the most powerful beginning to make room for your new life. Making space by letting go of "the old" creates opportunities to receive all that you already are and desire to be. Actually, your new life may already be present, waiting behind outdated possessions, thoughts, and behavior patterns that want to leave your life to make room for the new you.

To regenerate, recreate, or revitalize your life and self, let go of all that doesn't work anymore. This includes ways of relating with yourself and others, as well as emotional and mental patterns that are not supporting your longing. In other words, make sure that what you think and say to yourself (and others) is in alignment with your longing.

Ask yourself, What are the thoughts behind my feelings? What attitude do I entertain regularly? How do I wake up in the morning? What is my baseline emotion? Baseline emotions are feelings that you wake up to on a regular basis; they are a reliable indicator of where you live emotionally. One can live in peace, enjoyment, and neutrality and visit sadness, doubt, fear, or anger. Pay attention to where you live and what emotions you frequent. A heartfelt conversation with a trusted friend or a therapist might provide clarity as to what needs to be let go of and revised. Have fun with your mental and emotional housecleaning. You are making room for your new life.

Here is an example statement for letting go of all that is no longer needed:

> It is my choice to let go of all that which does not serve me anymore, easily and effortlessly—now!

Chapter 12

THE PRACTICE: PUTTING
IT ALL TOGETHER!

Here we are, almost to the end of our journey together. Certainly we have covered a lot of ground, and changes may already be happening in your life, moving you toward the wholeness you are truly longing for. But reading alone will not suffice. Now it's all about your practice. This is where you gain experience and get to know your own system. Remember this material came about out of years of practice. One step builds on the next. Enjoy every part of it.

When we consider the health of our aura in the game of creation, we have all of spiritual reality assisting us in making our dreams reality. In fact, we are designed that way to cocreate with the intelligence of life itself as who we are—as who *you* are specifically and uniquely. Never forget you already have your purpose inside of you and your longing is your road sign to help you recognize and fulfill your inner heart's dream. That is why you are here on earth right now—to live and thrive as who you are *uniquely*.

Pulling back the old layers takes time and patience. Give yourself the time, be kind to yourself in the process, have patience, be committed, and have fun.

Until one is committed, there is hesitancy, the chance to draw back, always ineffectiveness. Concerning all acts of initiative (and creation), there is one elementary truth, the ignorance of which kills countless ideas and splendid plans: that the moment one definitely commits oneself, then Providence moves too.

—Goethe

The following pages will give you a sample blueprint to access, track, and claim your aura and your chakra system. By systematically focusing on your chakras, the layers of your field, and your hara and core-star dimension, you'll be able to gradually heal your aura and enjoy yourself as who you are in the fullness of your being. Your personal practice is essential to the success in your life and will bring about the fulfillment of your longing. Your practice is the place to return to on a daily basis in order to build upon and refine what is to become the mastery of your craft—that which you choose to nurture within yourself, the thing that gives you joy, turns you on, and gives you life. You'll find yourself growing incrementally, building daily on your knowledge and experience while strengthening your hara. Your practice is progressive and accumulative, and over time it will become effortless. In part, this is because your personal practice is the place where your multidimensional support team can find and support you in your quest. The relationship with your team solidifies as you regularly harmonize in positive reality for the greater good of all, assuring the fulfillment of your purpose!

Unwavering commitment to your practice is a prerequisite for cocreation with the divine. This doesn't mean that you will be penalized for missing a day. But prioritizing marks a willingness to return to your chosen practice, which becomes your golden lotus seat. Even if daily challenges keep you for a day, your practice is your safety net to return to for a stronger connection with yourself. It will provide guidance, spiritual nurturing, and healing if needed. This is how you tap into and receive the generous gifts offered by your multidimensional support team. These gifts are granted and are yours for the taking. Ask and you shall receive! Master the skill of receiving into a fine art by *enjoying your practice*, as it will expand your core star and elevate your life to an expression of your true essence.

The Alignment of the Chakras and the Days of the Week

As it turns out, the days of the week and the chakras line up as a supportive system to help track your field no matter what day it is, meaning you can jump in at any time:

- Monday is about your first chakra, your first level of your field, and all about your physical reality.
- Tuesday is about your second chakra, your second level of your field, and your emotional body, as well as your creativity, your sexuality, and your emotional relationship with yourself.
- Wednesday is about your third chakra and third level of your field, your mental body, your belief system, and the celebration of your unique individuality.
- Thursday is the day of the heart chakra and the fourth level of your field; it's all about love and relationships, as well as healing the more distant past.
- Friday is about the fifth chakra and the fifth level of your field, how you use language to speak your personal creation into being, your voice of authority and your relationship with divine will.
- Saturday is about your sixth chakra and the sixth level of your field, your vision, divine love, art, beauty, and play.
- Sunday is the day of the seventh chakra and the seventh level of your field, the celebration of all that is, the whole mystery of life that you are part of, and the nurturing of your divine genius as it is expressed through your unique individuality.

Before you begin, decide how much time you are willing to

spend at a minimum each day to focus specifically on your aura. If you commit to ten minutes each day make sure you clear your schedule for that amount of time, plus a few minutes on either end (which would bring your total time to about fifteen minutes) so that you can fully relax into your practice. I recommend twenty minutes (plus five) a day of practice time to begin with for three months. Then reevaluate and add more time if desired. *Small changes are likely to accumulate into aha discovery moments that, over time, amount to lifestyle changes.* Be patient and kind with yourself, you are entering the new frontier of energetic presence and most of us are not trained to pay attention to the subtle feelings of our energy body, it might take some getting used to. Approaching your practice with a playful attitude assures your enjoyment and continuity.

What else are you committed to? To my knowledge, there is nothing that gets you through a challenging or confusing situation more quickly than knowing what your ultimate commitment is. If you are committed to positive reality, no matter what comes across your way, you'll look for a win-win outcome. If your ultimate commitment is the fulfillment of your longing, then you'll feel into your longing first, no matter what the situation is. Let your decision making be guided by feeling into your soul seat in the upper chest; this is where your longing resides.

To be clear, the following practice blueprint is geared to presence you in your aura—this increased awareness will enable you to take charge of your field for the purposes of healing yourself (becoming whole) and creating the life you desire. But any practice that you choose and fully commit yourself to will move you forward toward the fulfillment of your longing.

I have a dear friend who was struggling with all kinds of issues from the past that depleted and confused her body, mind, and field. As she was working with me, she also took up chanting with the Buddhists regularly for extended periods of time up to two hours a day. I witnessed how the chanting slowly cleared her aura, her mind, and her emotions. Her practice incrementally charged her field and her body and, finally, changed her mind-set to positive reality. I am truly impressed by her commitment to her practice and the undeniable positive change that it brought about in her life.

Monday: First Chakra

Monday is the day to focus on and to honor your first chakra. Be present to your body and how you are grounding your longing in physical reality. Here are the questions you may ask yourself on a Monday morning or at anytime on a Monday:

1. Do I live in harmony with my physical body?
2. What would serve my body best?
3. What does my body truly need?
4. What is the longing of my body?
5. Do I need to let go of anything food wise or activity wise?
6. Do I need to add anything like water, food, or exercise?
7. What kind of physical experience would make me truly happy?

First Chakra Practice and Statements

I recommend starting with a sitting practice for about ten to fifteen minutes, as that will give you the best chance to stay focused on your task. If you have more time, you might want to go into resting and healing practice after sitting. I recommend fifteen to twenty minutes for your resting or healing practice or more time if you have it available. Make sure that you are undisturbed for the duration of your practice. Have a timer on hand and set it, so you can forget about the time. Then initiate sacred space for your aura exploration or healing.

Statement to Set Up Sacred Healing Space for Yourself

> By the power invested in me, as to who and what I am, as a fully creative and conscious being of life itself, I declare this a sacred space for healing myself. I ask for truth, love, and healing on all levels of my being *and I ask in particular for healing awareness of my first chakra*. I invite my team, all the members of my team that I know [name them if you wish] and all those who are assisting me that I don't know. Thank you for your tireless service and for your presence, guidance, and assistance. I turn the healing (or practice) over to the Holy Spirit and to the greater good of all. And so it is! Amen.

As you are reclined and ready to receive your healing, direct your inner gaze—with your eyes closed but relaxed, look with your inner eyes at the inside of your body and field—to the location of your first chakra and keep it focused there. It is the space from your perineum down to your legs and feet in connection with the ground. Feel into the space of your first chakra as you keep your inner gaze on the vortex; it will most likely come alive with a sensation of heat and color. Say out loud or silently, "I am life; I am life itself!" Give yourself a few moments to feel the effect of this statement on your body and field. Then repeat, "I am life; I am life itself and as that life that I am, I am supported by life fully and completely as who and what I am."

Allow for the reverberations of this statement to wash over you. Pay attention to the subtle sensations and feelings in your body, legs, and pelvis. Tingling, movement of energy, and perceived temperature changes can all be part of your experience. At times, there may be an awareness of minor pain sensations moving through your body and your legs. This is most likely a clearing. If this happens, support yourself and your body by saying this statement: "I allow it!" Then relax and allow. Most likely, it will move through in due time.

Give yourself permission to see and feel all that there is for you to know while you keep your focus on your first chakra. What are you perceiving? Do you see a color? Does your energy level change? Are you more relaxed or energized? Perhaps you'll see the spinning red vortex that is your first chakra or feel a movement in the area of it. Or you might just go into nice relaxation. It's all good and beneficial to the health of your first chakra. Regular attention will make the difference in knowing and changing your first chakra for the better. And because it is the foundation for your good health, you can't visit it too often.

Tuesday: Second Chakra

Tuesday is all about your second chakra—your creativity, your sexuality, and your emotional relationship with yourself, as well as the quantity and quality of your life-force energy.

Here are the questions to ask yourself on Tuesdays:

1. What is my emotional baseline? In other words, how do I feel when I wake most mornings?
2. Do I feel the good feelings of what it means to be me? (I call it being present to the yumminess of my being.)
3. What is my emotional longing?
4. Do I have unexpressed emotions gnawing at me?
5. Is my inner relationship with myself kind and supportive to myself?
6. Do I enjoy my own creativity?
7. Is my emotional energy plentiful and positive?

The second chakra has a front and back aspect. To begin with, we will focus on the middle of your lower belly, where the front and back meet in the vertical power current. Any time on Tuesday is a chance to tune into your second chakra. I can't stress enough the importance of continuity, as it helps you to become familiar with a particular chakra.

Start your practice by setting up sacred space. Use the same invocation as before but change it to explore and heal the second chakra:

> By the power invested in me, as to who and what I am, as a fully creative and conscious being of life itself, I declare this a sacred space for healing myself. I ask for truth, love, and healing on all levels of my being *and ask in particular for a healing awareness of my second chakra.* I invite the presence of my team, all the members of my team that I know [name them if you wish] and all those who are assisting me that I don't know. Thank you for your tireless service and for your presence, guidance, and assistance. I turn the healing (or practice) over to the Holy Spirit and the greater good of all. And so it is! Amen.

Direct your inner gaze to the location of your second chakra, which is located about two to three inches below your belly button, in the center. The back aspect of the second chakra is centered at the sacrum. Focus your inner gaze in the center of your lower belly where the front and back of the second chakra join together. Feel into the space of your second chakra and keep your inner gaze on the center; it might come alive with sensation, heat, and color. The ideal color is a bright warm orange.

Say out loud or silently, "I feel myself as who and what I am—only!" Give yourself a few moments to feel the effect of this statement on your body and field. Then repeat, "I feel myself as who and what I am only; there is no need to change anything!" Then relax into this truth.

Indeed, there is no need to change anything right now. Be present to what is. Feel, experience, and witness. As you are focusing your inner gaze gently in the center of your lower belly, you are building vital energy by being present in your second chakra. You may be releasing emotions that have been stored here and are now becoming unblocked. If this happens, let your emotions flow. Saying "I allow it!" will help you surrender into the experience. Taking mental or voice notes (with your phone) will be helpful in tracking your progress.

Wednesday: Third Chakra

Wednesday is the day of your third chakra. To tune into your mental body, become conscious of your driving belief systems and honor and celebrate your unique individuality.

Questions to ask yourself on a Wednesday:

1. What do I feel when I tune into my third chakra?
2. What are my God-given gifts or talents?
3. Are my thoughts honoring my longing?
4. Do I make my important decisions in life based on fear?
5. Do my beliefs help me create the life I love?
6. Do I feel positively connected to the world and to others?
7. Am I willing to do what it takes to take care of myself in all aspects of my life?

For your practice on Wednesdays, initiate sacred space using your invocation with a specific focus on your third chakra. Then gently direct your inner gaze to your solar plexus, which is the location of your third chakra in the front; the rear aspect is located in the middle back between your kidneys. Ideally, the chakra is a bright yellow. A darker version may indicate stagnation but is nothing to worry about; instead, simply observe. Say out loud, "I honor and celebrate my unique individuality." Then feel how this statement affects your body and field.

The third chakra governs all of your vital organs in the area of your solar plexus—your liver, gallbladder, pancreas, spleen, stomach, and parts of the small intestine. It is bright yellow in color when healthy and gets muddy-looking when blocked or distorted. Pushing too much mental energy through this center will stress and distort the third chakra. Distortions tend to intensify if the adjoining chakras, above and below, are not functioning properly.

Tears in the protective membrane that cover each chakra are common; these energy leaks are draining and physically irritating. If you become aware of a tear or leak, keep your gentle attention on the spot and say, "I allow it!" That will move things in the right direction.

In any case, don't push against it. Stay present to what is and notice any thoughts or images arising on the screen of your mind. Practice compassion and forgiveness for your own experience; judgment is not helpful. If you get stuck anywhere, ask your team for help.

Thursday: The Heart Chakra

Thursday is the day of the heart chakra. This fourth level of your aura is all about relationships. It's about God; life in general; and your relationship with other human beings, past and present. Your heart chakra is the bridge between spiritual and physical reality and holds the key for deeper healing.

Here are the questions to ask yourself on Thursdays:

1. What is the state of my emotional heart?
2. What is the state of my physical heart?
3. Are my relationships fulfilling to me?
4. Is my general outlook in life positive?
5. Am I overly or regularly critical of others?
6. Do I have enough joy in my life?
7. What is the longing of my heart today?

Your practice on Thursdays is *centered in your chest*. Initiate sacred space, direct your inner gaze to your heart, and feel what resides in your heart chakra. Say out loud to your body, your bones, your tissues, and your being, "I am love! I am love unto my body, and I am love unto my being!" Then allow and receive the effect of your statement.

The color of the heart chakra, when open and fully expressed, is emerald green. In the front, it is about the quality of love you give to others and the world around you; in the back, it is about your willingness to receive the world as a loving place for who you are. The front of your heart chakra governs the lungs and thymus, while the back of your heart center affects the thoracic spine and shoulder area. The sensitive area at the upper heart located at the sternum, called the soul seat, is where your longing resides. If it is alive, it will have you glowing and move you toward the fulfillment of your inner heart's dream. Or it may be shrouded, in which case it would feel foggy, dark, or burdened. When you gaze upon your own heart, front or back, do you feel open and warm, or do you feel closed, tense, and protective?

Whatever your experience, allow it. You are gathering vital information and changing your heart energy by being present to your heart chakra. In addition, focusing on your heart energy widens the door to the spiritual aspect of your being, which is already connected to your multidimensional support team. Hence, with the assistance of your MDST, your healing can be greatly accelerated. Be gentle and kind to yourself!

At this point of your practice, you may have built up to a dynamic healing wave, bringing about exciting and positive changes in all areas of your life for you to enjoy and claim as your new reality.

A new level of complexity is added on the fourth level of the field, as it holds memory from the distant past that may color your everyday experience. Unresolved past-life memory is stored on the fourth level of the field, which is governed by the heart chakra. If a past life is activated, it can affect any part of the physical body with mild to intense physical pain. In addition, chronic emotional, mental, or spiritual suffering can be signs of a past-life overlay at work. These unresolved past-life occurrences are more difficult to detect and are often medically diagnosed as chronic and/or mysterious. In other words, after thorough examination, the findings remain inconclusive, and from a medical perspective, no good reason for the condition presented can be found.

Clearing past-life trauma is a high-level healing skill and best done under the guidance of an experienced professional healer.

Unconditional love, forgiveness, and compassion toward yourself and others are key when seeking to clear a past-life trauma. While some astral matter will clear naturally with forgiveness, a guide and/or witness may be needed to help you release longstanding and more difficult past-life traumas from your body and your field.

Friday: Fifth Chakra

Friday is about your fifth chakra. It involves your relationship with authority, how you speak your creation into being, and cocreation with divine will for the greater good of all.

Questions to ask yourself on a Friday are:

1. Is my will in alignment with my longing?
2. Does my everyday language support what I desire to create?
3. What is divine will/my will, today right now?
4. Am I able to ask for what I want or need in life and from others?
5. Do I trust in a greater support system beyond myself?
6. Do I believe that *the greater good of all* incudes my wants and needs?
7. Am I present to my own voice when I speak, and what do I sound like to myself?

Set up your Friday practice session *to observe, clear, and charge your fifth chakra by focusing on the center of your throat.* Focus your inner gaze on the center of your throat and say out loud, "It is my choice to align my will with divine will, and I know that I will be served in the very best and most elegant way, which naturally includes my greater good." Then observe what happens. If you perceive color, it may be sky blue or cobalt blue. The chakra itself is sky blue when healthy and opens to the fifth level of the field, which is a spacious cobalt blue that is holding the blueprint for all things physical. It looks like a negative photograph with white space for that which makes up any part of the body, enclosed in spacious, calm cobalt blue.

Your fifth chakra governs your voice box, thyroid, upper esophagus in the front, and cervical spine in the back. Your voice box and vocal cords, together with your will and emotions, modulate the sound of your voice. Your voice, your intention, and the choice of your words help to shape your fifth chakra and determine the quality of your creation. No matter who you are addressing, the shortest distance is from your mouth to your ear. So listen closely to the sound of your voice, the choice of your words, and how it feels *to you* when you are expressing yourself. The fifth chakra holds the balance between your heart, your longing, and your reasoning head.

Then one day when you are practicing, your heart will be open; you will be present to your longing; and you, my dear friend, will have a vision. To go about manifesting your dream in practical ways, ask your MDST team to help you. Ask and you shall receive is the motto of your fifth chakra, and it is a true statement as far as guidance is concerned. You have to ask in order to receive. Otherwise, for your MDST to get involved would be an interference with your free will. So remember, a complaint is not a request. When your request also serves the greater good of all, chances are, you'll move *like magic* to the front of the line, to merge with the supportive realm of the greater good for all. Trust that you have been heard and complete your request by saying these two magical words—thank you! Don't undermine your request with doubt, but hold up your end of the deal by trusting in your honest heartfelt request.

Saturday: Sixth Chakra

Saturday is the day of the sixth chakra; and it's all about divine love, beauty, art, inspiration, celebration, and vision. Saturday is your day to play and to enjoy and celebrate life with loved ones or in your own good company—right after your practice of course.

Here are the questions to ask yourself on Saturday:

1. What would I like to enjoy today?
2. Who would I like to connect with today?
3. What would inspire me?
4. Is there something to celebrate?
5. Is there something I am curious about that I would like to explore?
6. Is there enough beauty in my life?
7. Am I present to my vision and living it as who I am now?

As usual, initiate sacred space for your practice and focus on your sixth chakra in the center of your head. You can venture from here to the front or the back aspect of your sixth chakra as you advance in your practice. But for now, stay in the center of your head where these two aspects come together in the vertical power current. The color of the sixth chakra is indigo or purple. There is a calm place between our ears and behind the center of both eyes; this is your golden lotus seat. Here you claim dominion over your life by being present to your thoughts and observing and letting them pass by like clouds in the sky. Become present to your vision and what you are projecting onto the screen of life.

When you feel fully present, say out loud, "I am divinely loved!" Then feel the effect of your statement on your body and field. Repeat as desired.

Your thoughts and visions, together with your feelings, become your manifestations. Everything we see, use, or enjoy, except nature of course, was first someone's inner vision. Make sure your projection onto the big screen of life is a creation that you'll want to receive and enjoy.

Your sixth chakra, together with the seventh chakra, governs your eyes, brain, and endocrine system by way of your pituitary and pineal gland. Provided you stick with your practice, you'll be able to take charge of your endocrine system to bring balance to your hormones. So practice daily with joy, and stay tuned, as this advanced high-level healing skill is the exciting subject of my next book.

Sunday: Seventh Chakra

Sunday is the day of your seventh chakra and the seventh level of your field. It is the day to honor your divine genius of God. Maximize, celebrate, and enjoy your God-given gifts by fully receiving them.

Questions to explore on Sundays are:

1. How do I best serve God, source, or the greater good of all?
2. What is the collective dream or vision that I am holding for my family or for the world?
3. How does divine will express itself through me?
4. What is my heart's desire, not only for myself but also for the world?
5. How do I enjoy my unique being or my individuality?
6. Who or what makes me feel most like myself?
7. Physically, what makes me feel like heaven on earth?

- Set up your practice on Sunday as usual with your invocation and then begin by focusing on the center of your head where your sixth and seventh chakra come together in the vertical power current. If you are able to perceive it, the color of the crown chakra is white opalescent gold. Say out loud, "It is my choice, to fully receive my divine genius of God as the unique individual that I am—now!" Continue to be present in the center of your head and observe what happens for a few minutes. Feel your connection to all that is, was, and will be. You are part of all that, the whole mystery of life. Let yourself merge if you wish, but make sure you come back to who you are as the unique individual that you are.

- Then move your attention down to the center of your throat where the fifth chakra opens to the fifth level of the field. Feel the fabric of divine will around you in support of your dreams and for the greater good of all. Do you wish to participate? If so, state it by saying, "I align my will with divine will, and I know that I will be served in the very best way that includes my greater good, needs, and wants. And that is my choice!" Then observe any changes in your field or consciousness.

- Next, move to the center of your chest to feel your heart chakra and the fourth level of your field. Say out loud to your bones, tissues, and your being, "I am love. I am love unto myself. And I am love unto my body, past and present!" Then observe and receive the influx of positive love energy in your body and your field. Stay in your heart to bask in the glow and send out rays of loving kindness to those who come to mind. Enjoy!

- Then focus on your third chakra at your solar plexus, which opens to the third level of your field. Keep your gaze at this center while radiating with confidence the vibrant light of your unique individuality. Let yourself shine like the sun and be like the sun to those around you. Say out loud, "I honor and celebrate my unique individuality." Enjoy your own presence, the gifts of your personality, and all that makes you uniquely you. It will help those around you to feel themselves as who and what they truly are.

- Moving your inner gaze down to the center of your belly, your second chakra, which opens to the second level of your field and your emotional body, say out loud, "I feel myself as who and what I am only!" Let yourself sink in and bask in the good feelings of what it means to be you! Enjoy the yumminess of your being!

- Last but not least, bring your focus to your first chakra at your perineum, which is the counterpart to your seventh chakra. When these two centers come together in harmony, you can experience heaven on earth as a physical reality.

It just feels so good to be alive! Say out loud, "I am life! I am life itself! And I am the magic of life. Therefore, life supports me exactly as who and what I am, especially in the fulfillment of my inner heart's dream."

Let yourself be that vibrant life you desire; allow it. You are it—the gift and the giver. Give yourself to life and celebrate who you are by enjoying all aspects of your being. You are a vital part of all that is, was, and will be—the whole magical, mystical thing called life. You are here, and it is now! Choose to harmonize with life itself. Feel the beat, the pulsing of your sacred human heart in harmony with all others everywhere. This is life, your life, your body, and your creation. Have fun and enjoy!

By following this practice, you'll get to know and heal your aura while building your avatar body over time. Your avatar body is your physical body in harmony with your aura and your hara, expressing your core star reality in the here and now. A fully integrated aura provides the template for your spirit being to be physicalized. Your spirit being knows how to create and cocreate with the intelligence of life itself and thrives when in service to the greater good of all. The avatar knows how to care for its body, avails itself of all possibilities for health and wholeness naturally, effortlessly, and in harmony with the inner and outer world.

Success and Healing with Spiritual Surgery

Lastly, on these next pages, I want to give you an idea of how spiritual healing or, in this case, spiritual surgery can assist in healing challenging physical issues, even from a distance. As this is an advanced healing practice, I have put it last, mostly as an example of what is possible when one harmonizes with spiritual reality for the greater good of all. In this case, spiritual surgery helped Anna's mom heal from a relentless cancer issue that had required the removal of her nose. This story is about the final reconstruction of her new nose that, at first, would not take.

The operation was finally successful after application of spiritual surgery before another attempt of the actual physical surgery. It was all done over distance.

In spiritual surgery the area of concern is addressed through the template of the fifth level of the field, with help of a spiritual surgical healing team (light beings). These are like the operating teams in physical reality. From the fifth level of the field, the rest of the aura can be accessed in order to make needed healing adjustments. A surgical healing team is assembled according to the specific needs of a client and directed by the complaint or the condition. The preparatory healing meditation before a spiritual surgery sends out the call and requests a team with the needed specifications. Each etheric healing team seems to be individually assembled accordingly and specific as to what is needed at the time.

Anna had had excellent results with her distant healing series, including spiritual surgery, and therefore, she wanted to help her mother. She asked me if I could help her mom, who was recovering from skin cancer on her face. The tip of her nose had been taken off and was to be reconstructed with grafts from her ears and arms. The operation had a 50 percent chance of being successful. She had already undergone a series of surgeries that were not entirely successful, and another one was scheduled.

To complicate the matter, Anna's mother did not really believe in healing modalities other then traditional Western medicine. Anna suggested a stealth operation first, if it was to happen at all.

I told Anna that I would get back to her after I had determined if it was ethical for me to work on her mother without her direct permission. Consulting with my peers and looking into the matter, I came to the conclusion that it was ethical to work with her mom from a distance, with authorization by her daughter. Anna had asked for her mom's permission to work with her herself, as she was also a trained healer in another modality. I thought it best for her mom to receive the healing in the middle of the night when she was at rest. Receiving the healing at night gave her a good chance of integrating the work without the distractions of a busy daytime hospital. She did not have to be awake for the *distance healing* to be effective.

To begin with, I looked at her field from a distance and saw that some basic healing had to take place before the situation with her nose could be addressed. The cancer and the treatment had taken a toll on her. Her grounding was missing, and the rest of her aura needed help recovering from the ongoing cancer ordeal. We scheduled a series of healing sessions, which were to take place at midnight for her mom who resides in the United Kingdom. I was happy to work out the time difference and excited about the opportunity to be of service in this matter. I really wanted it to be successful.

At first, Anna's mom was skeptical, and I had the feeling she just went along to please her daughter. But after she had received a couple of healing sessions, her state of health and outlook improved so dramatically that she herself agreed and asked for the healing. I was told that she was looking forward to the sessions. I could see from a distance that dramatic improvements were taking place in her field and physical body.

Anna shared her mom's progress with me by forwarding the e-mails that her mom had sent to her. Then, in a phone conversation before a vital transplant operation, Anna shared with her mom that, in fact, a healer other then herself was working with her. By that time, we all had come to an agreement that the healing sessions were good and beneficial. And with that, the way was cleared to help her in more detail.

The next scheduled operation was crucial for the success of the transplant to fully take hold, as it had failed more than once before. It was a necessary rerouting of the arteries to ensure blood supply to the tissue that had been transplanted from the ears and arms to the nose.

The distant healing session was scheduled for the night before the physical operation.

When in spiritual surgery, I am part of a team—essential and central to the etheric surgeons, as they pass through me for all that is needed. This includes instruments of all types, some of which exist in physical form and some that are not yet in physical form, as they have not yet been developed. I hold open a corridor and become the go-between, negotiating etheric and physical realities.

In spiritual surgery, I am a bridge and a corridor for entire etheric surgical teams to work through me. Knowing this would have to be a spiritual surgery, I assembled my team in a preparatory meditation. Or rather, I joined the etheric team that had already gathered, ready for the task. I was late by twenty minutes. Much to my surprise, a whole team, bigger than usual, was waiting for me to start by the time I sat down for the healing. There was much excitement in the air. I felt honored and privileged to be part of this team. As I was the go-between, bridging the etheric to the physical, they could not start without me and were indeed waiting. I could clearly see that Anna's mom having come into full agreement made a difference, as part of her personal team was present too.

Much as would happen if a surgical team were to walk into a physical operating room, everyone went to work with intense focus. One by one, all moved into place. I could feel energetic arms and hands overlaying mine and etheric instruments that were being passed down through my head, my arms, and hands. My inner eyes focused on the etheric template, and I saw the whole operation take place through all of the levels of the aura. Everything that was to happen in the physical operation, which was scheduled in a few hours' time, was being done on the etheric realm in detailed preparation. Watching and participating in the entire sacred healing event was exhilarating. After it was complete, I felt spent in a happy way. The next day, I was tired, no doubt from this tremendously focused healing session. My multidimensional support team assured me that the operation was successful. I was waiting for hopeful news from Anna's mom.

Days later, I got a distressed message from Anna letting me know that her mom was worried. The nose was still black, and the doctors had put her on notice that it might not take again. I took a moment to go inside and consult with my guides about the matter; I was told that it was essential to hold steadfast, to remain positive, and to keep the faith. I was also told that the nose was going to turn pink shortly and become pinker day by day. I related this to Anna, which she shared with her mom.

A few days later, I got news from Anna that her mom was overjoyed; her nose had indeed turned pink, and the transplant was holding. This was much to the surprise of the surgeons who performed the physical operation. They filed into her room in order to confirm the news about the transplant holding and her new pink nose.

In my healing practice, spiritual surgery has proven itself to be ultimately supportive for my clients in preparation for upcoming medical procedures, as well as a postoperative option to aid recovery from surgery. Healing time and pain can be significantly reduced with this advanced healing modality, and in some cases, the success of a medical procedure has been greatly supported and even ensured.

Other uses for spiritual surgery are to relieve joint pain or organ pain, as well as mysterious and sometimes chronic pain.

I have gone from one spiritual surgery to another within hours, with entirely different teams present. Spiritual surgery is a unique experience for me as the healer and for the recipient. When I work with clients in person, sometimes they inform me about the experience that they are having, if they happen to be awake and able to track the healing. Often they can feel and sense the sensation of having their template adjusted, pulled, vacuumed, and even cut. Slight discomfort might be part of the experience, but mostly they are benign sensations of healing in progress. This can be exciting as well as affirmative for the client, as it is most powerful to have a direct experience that one can recall as part of the healing. However, a spiritual surgery is no less effective if a client is asleep during the healing.

A resting and integration period is almost always recommended and needed. The length of recovery time depends on the degree of intervention. Sometimes a procedure might have multiple steps to it, and therefore, multiple spiritual surgeries are needed.

Epilogue

In the course of writing this book, I became increasingly aware of another longing deep within my heart—the longing to be with my beloved one. When I began writing *Heart Flame Healing*, I had been single for a while and rather enjoying it for the most part. But as my book was about the deep longing of the heart, I felt my desire to share my life with my beloved one and decided to be present to this sacred longing of mine, to feel it deeply and to nurture it.

I remembered a quote by one of my teachers: "Whatever you are longing for is also longing for you—equally." Knowing this to be true, I started praying for my beloved one to come and be with me. I set aside five minutes each morning to sit for the relationship I so desired. I just sat in silence dedicating the time, being peaceful and in positive reality expectancy. I knew that, if I felt my longing in positive reality—meaning if I held space for the fulfillment of my desire—that I would surely meet my beloved one. I did this for a few weeks, and when Valentine's Day arrived, I decided to spend the lover's holiday honoring my sacred longing. I cleared my schedule so I could enjoy the whole day—hiking, making delicious food, and spending the day in honor of my longing to be fulfilled. Throughout the day, I thought about the qualities I so desired in my future partner. But I could not fully commit to the "shopping list" as a practice, so I decided to let go of it.

Still I kept thinking, *What would qualify my future love?* Finally I knew that our connection would have to be at the level of our hara and core star dimension. That way, our intentions for our life together would match with each other. As the day came to a close, I felt wonderful. Dancing by myself in my loft apartment, I chanted poetry to my beloved. While gently moving my body, I asked the universe to bring us together, to match me with the one who's hara and core star matched mine. A moment later, I felt a sensation in my lower abdomen. I recognized his hara energetically connecting with mine. I noticed how strong it was and felt the dynamic presence of his being close to mine. Following that, I had a few dreams that let me know that my beloved was on his way. The dreams were detailed in such a way that I knew his height and body type. We met just two months after that via an online dating service. We have been living, loving, and growing together as a couple ever since.

One of the most surprising aspects of our connection is that my beloved loves my food. Now as you know, my diet is quite extreme. What are the chances? He takes photos of nearly all my meals and collects them in a file. Perhaps to be published next?

My diet is even more refined now as I come to the conclusion of writing *Heart Flame Healing* than it was when I started writing, but I took the challenge and mastered my food prep skills into a vegetarian culinary art. Moving it all into positive reality, I have given up any lament about my body's reaction to sugar, salt, fruit, or grain. I know that my body's condition serves me best and to the highest degree. It perfectly supports my work. My diet not only provides the nutrition that is best for my body, but it also keeps my frequency high enough to make my healing work and the connection with my team effortless. As such, the unique requirements of my body (or allergic reaction to sugar, salt, and grains) serve the greater good of all, and I am grateful for it.

***

168

Thank you for reading *Heart Flame Healing*. Know that you are always guided—guidance is available for the asking, no matter what the circumstances of your life. Your multidimensional support team is standing by.

If you want to get in touch with me, please email me at inana@fastmail.fm

Appendix 1

Healing Statements and Exercises

Chakra Healing Statements

First chakra. I am life! I am life itself!

Second chakra. I feel myself as who and what I am only.

Third chakra. I honor and celebrate my unique individuality.

Heart chakra. I am love unto my body, and I am love unto myself.

Fifth chakra. I align my will with divine will, and I know that I will be served in the best and most elegant way that includes my needs and wants.

Sixth chakra. I am divinely loved.

Seventh chakra. I am one with "all that is," the whole mystery of life.

Exercise to Begin Clearing Your First Chakra

- The statement is, "I am life. I am life itself."
- Take about ten minutes for this practice.
- Sit with a straight spine with your feet on the ground.
- Observe, relax, and feel into the ebb and flow of your breath.
- Direct your inner gaze (with your eyes closed) to your perineum, where the narrow tip of your first chakra comes into the vertical power current. The wide part of the chakra opens to the feet and the ground beneath you.
- What do you feel here (from the pubic bone down to the earth)?
- What do your legs and feet feel like? Are your legs alive with energy? Can you feel your toes?
- Keeping your inner gaze on your perineum and your breath steady, relax into the area of your first chakra.
- Do you see a color? Do you feel a movement of energy? Do you feel calm or agitated?
- If you have a question about your first chakra, ask it out loud. You may get an answer immediately or in the following hours. The question may be, "What does my first chakra need most at this time?"
- End your session by saying, "I am life, I am life itself," and then, "Thank you," out loud.

The ideal color of the first chakra is a bright red. It can also be dark red or muddy brown when distorted. When you are starting out you may not feel or see much. Don't be discouraged, even if you don't get anything at first, the practice itself will improve your first health chakra health for the better and you'll get more detailed information about your first chakra as you continue to practice.

The Golden Liquid Bowl of Fire (for second chakra clearing)

Visualize your pelvic bowl as an actual energetic bowl—a container filled with a life-giving liquid fire. See the red of the first chakra;

here are the embers out of which the warm orange flames of the second chakra rise. These beautiful, vital orange flames are warm rather than hot and deeply nourishing. At the top licks the yellow flame of the healthy mind, bringing understanding to the emotions that are being processed. This is followed by the green of the heart chakra. And finally, the violet flame of divine love consumes and purifies the rest, leaving only pure creative energy for greater enjoyment of your being.

- As you begin this exercise, say out loud to yourself, "I feel myself as who and what I am only. There is no need to change anything." By doing so, you give yourself permission to feel all there is to feel without judgment. There is nothing to do about it; just observe and allow.
- Move to visualize your golden liquid fire bowl. Notice the shape and size of it. See the hue of red that makes up the flame rising from the first chakra, and then see it turning to a warm nurturing orange.
- Feel the warmth rising from the flames warming your pelvis. Allow yourself to be with whatever comes up. Be your own witness and observe while continuing to breathe gently into your pelvis.
- Sit in your golden liquid bowl of fire for at least five minutes a day, and your emotional life will change for the better. Enjoy the warmth of the flames and their nurturing quality as you witness purification over time. This should feel good and calming to you!
- Be patient with yourself as you do this for the first time; you might have to move through some emotional material that has been stored in the pelvis and that is now given a way to clear itself.
- Give it the time it takes. Trust the process. It will get better and more enjoyable each time you go back to it. You are cultivating a stronger, more resilient second chakra.

Exercise to Begin Clearing Your Third Chakra

Give yourself ten minutes for this exercise. Sit and breathe naturally into the area of your solar plexus. If you have disturbances or complaints in your third chakra area, to begin with, feel into it in detail. Where exactly to you feel the energy leak or disturbance in you body? Notice if the feeling is predominantly physical, emotional, or mental.

- The statement is, "I allow it."
- Then with your eyes closed focus on the area specifically where you feel a disturbance. Stay present to yourself right in this area. Listen to your body. Ask yourself, What is needed here? Are there any foods that I am eating that are not benefiting me? And what are they?
- What comes to mind after you ask that question? What do you see or think of?
- You can also ask yourself, What foods that I am eating presently no longer serve my health and well-being at this point?
- What is the emotion that is present as you feel into this area? Do you feel anger, fear, or resentment? And if so, who is this inner dispute with? What needs to be communicated, forgiven, and to let go of?
- When you listen to inner dialogue, is it self-supporting or tearing you down? Can you be your own inner best friend while talking to yourself internally?
- Remember that you're whole and complete in your own right already. Letting go of trauma is a process. Be gentle and kind in your inner conversation with yourself.
- Before you get up, please say, "I honor and celebrate my unique individuality!" It is your closing statement for this exercise! How does it make you feel to say this?

Exercise to Clear and Heal the Heart Chakra

Take at least ten minutes. Sit and focus on the natural flow of breath in the center of your chest.

- The statement is, "I am love."
- Then, keeping your focus on the center of your chest, connect with the natural ebb and flow of your breath. What do you feel here?
- Are you experiencing joy or sadness when you focus at the center of your chest? Do you feel bright and energized or a sense of dullness? Whatever it is, allow it!
- What persons come to mind as you do this? What is the story or issue that arises? Is there someone or something that needs to be forgiven? If you are present to blame or anger against someone or even yourself, it's a sign that forgiveness is needed.
- To forgive, say this, "It is my choice to forgive [name of person (for example, my mother)] completely for [name what happened (for example, abandoning me when ….)]. I forgive [her or him], as well as life, God, myself, and nature now, completely. And that is my choice now! Thank you."
- Then sit and wait a few minutes for things to clear. Each person or incident requires a separate statement.

For best results do one incident or one person at the time. Pushing yourself to go faster does not increase results. However, being kind and gentle to yourself does make for best results.

Exercise to Begin Healing Your Fifth Chakra, or Throat Chakra

- Take at least ten minutes. Sit for a few moments in silence, breathing naturally while tuning into your throat chakra.
- The statement is, "I align my will with divine will."

175

- Physically, how is the area around your throat feeling? Does it feel open or blocked in someway?
- Do you express yourself easily? Or are you hesitant or shy?
- Generally, are you speaking your truth? Or are you holding back?
- What is the quality of your communication like, with others, with source, and with yourself?
- How do you speak your creation into being?
- How easy is it for you to ask for help?
- If there is one thing that needs to be expressed now, what is it and to whom? If there is one thing that you need help with in your life right now, who can you ask?
- To invite spiritual guidance and assistance, try this. Say, "It is my choice and my request for guidance and help in this matter. [State the issue in brief.] I give thanks for any and all help, your guidance and assistance. Thank you!"
- Then sit and let it go. You may receive some information right away or in the next hour or day. Trust the process.

The motto of the fifth chakra is "ask and you shall receive." But remember, asking for what you want is key.

Exercise to Claim Your Sixth Chakra

- Take at least ten minutes for this meditation.
- The statement is, "I am divinely loved and guided."
- To begin, sit and observe your natural breath for a few moments.
- Then shift your focus to your third eye between your brows and the center of your head in line with your ears.
- Notice, how does this area of your sixth chakra feel? Does it feel clear or foggy, blocked, or jumbled? How does the back of your head feel?What are you envisioning for your life?
- Is what you are projecting onto the screen of your life in alignment with your longing? And do your daily actions

match it? In other words, do you support your vision by moving into action and putting in motion and manifesting the life you desire?

- Now, in order to claim more of your sixth chakra function, visualize yourself—a very small version of your essence self (all the best parts of yourself)—sitting inside the center of your own head on a golden lotus flower. Here, you are in charge of your thoughts and of directing your life. Keep breathing and imagine light radiating from your essence self, filling your head with light.
- Sit until you feel clear enough and then ask yourself this question: What is the next step in realizing my vision?
- Be willing to receive information on that next step. You only have to know your next step to move forward. When this step is in motion in your life, ask for the next step to fulfill your vision.
- Know that you are guided, divinely loved, and divinely supported in fulfilling your vision.

Exercise to Open, Clear, and Expand Your Seventh Chakra

- The statement is, "I am a vital part of all that is."
- Sit for about ten minutes (with a straight back if you can).
- Visualize the earth underneath your feet (no matter where you are).
- Breathing naturally, visualize and feel earth energy come up through your feet and legs into your pelvis, up to your heart, and through your neck. Feel and see it expanding into a spiral out the top of your head.
- Stay firmly grounded even as you open to the vastness of the universe through your seventh chakra.
- The first chakra is the counterpart to the seventh chakra. Feel the grounding support of the earth as you open to the expanding consciousness of your seventh chakra, connecting you to all that is—which you are an integral

part of—the whole mystery of life. You are connected to and part of the all of it!

- Feel the uniqueness of your being in connection with all that is. Soak it up.

General Healing Invocation

I [your name] declare this a sacred space for a healing for myself.

I ask for truth, love, and healing on all levels of being and, in particular, for this issue at hand [state issue]. (To begin with, you might ask for a nourishing twenty-minute nap that has you feeling refreshed and inspired. It's best to start out simple so that you can track your experience and then graduate to more complex healings.)

I ask for the highest level of healing, and I give thanks for the healing I am about to receive.

I welcome and invite assistance and guidance in relationship to the issue at hand.

I give thanks for the presence of my multidimensional support team and for the team's guidance and assistance.

I turn the healing over to the Holy Spirit for the greater good of all.

And so it is. It is done. Thank you/ Amen

And to receive more deeply, it is my choice to relax deeply and to receive this healing that is coming my way now. And that is my choice!

Healing Skill: Statement for a Healing Walk

Here is your statement to initiate your healing walk to wake up your first chakra:

It is my choice and intention to move, to wake up, and to enliven my body. I declare this walk to be a

healing event to wake up my first chakra. And that
is my choice!

You can expand upon that command as you wish, and you may want to invite members of your MDST to walk with you for guidance on a specific matter.

Healing Skill: Resting (Also see chapter 5, "The Art of Resting and Receiving.")

It is best to do this practice after a walk. Take ten to fifteen minutes to rest on your back. Give your body the space and permission to receive all the good you have generated during your walk. You can also practice without walking beforehand.

- Lie on your back, perhaps with a pillow under your knees and a support for your neck.
- Make sure you are absolutely comfortable, cover your eyes, and let go.
- With the first few breaths, let go of all your thoughts; breathe them out and come into this moment.
- Feel the ebb and flow of your breath in your chest.
- Then become present to your limbs, hands, and feet. Let them rest on the bed or floor. Feel the support underneath you and receive it fully.
- Then become present to the skin of your face and how your breath flows in through your nose and mouth, down into your lungs, and to the heart.
- Now take the path of your newly oxygenated blood flowing through, nurturing your brain organs and tissues.
- Connect with your heartbeat and observe your breath.
- There is nothing you have to do for the moment other than feel life pulsing in your chest and breathing you.
- Let life breathe you! This alone can be a revelation in healing. Try it; it can change your life.

Forgiveness Invocation

(Sometimes one has to be willing to just say the words.)

> Even though I don't know all of the details of this
> unexplained pain or sensation I am
> experiencing, it is my choice to forgive it all—
> no matter when it originated, where it originated,
> or why.
> No matter who was involved or how long it was
> endured.
> it is my choice to forgive it all, now, completely!
> Including life, God, myself, and anyone who was
> involved, as well as nature,
> circumstances, and my body, I forgive all now
> completely!
> That is my choice, and thank you!

Be present to the location of the pain sensation as you say it; open up with your consciousness right inside of it. Say the statement and be silent for a few minutes after it to allow for the release or more information to rise. You might have to say it a few times for different sensations.

Here is another sample invocation for a specific task, in this case for writing:

> By the power invested in me, as a fully creative
> being of God in multidimensional reality, manifesting
> in the here and now, without limits, I declare this
> a sacred space for establishing divine contact and
> communication with my team, muses, and guides
> for the purpose of writing *Heart Flame Healing* [for
> the purpose of sleep, healing, inspiration, or any
> other specific task can be said in place of writing].

Thank you for your presence, guidance, and assistance!

Please help me to put into language the highest truth of what I know so well so that others may have a direct experience and feel the truth of these words.

I turn the writing session over to the Holy Spirit and to the greater good of all.

Thank you. It is done!

Amen.

Unmerging and Letting Go What is No Longer Needed

To *unmerge*, say:

> I allow all that which is not me to pass through me without residue, and I pass it on with a blessing of ease and grace—now!

Follow up with:

> I feel myself as who and what I am—only!"

To *let go of all that is no longer needed*, say:

> It is my choice to let go of all old emotional patterns that do not serve me anymore, easily and effortlessly. That is my choice—now!

Appendix 2

GLOSSARY FOR HEART FLAME HEALING

astral body. An aspect of our being. An astral body can live simultaneously in the physical and nonphysical world and is governed by the heart chakra. Past-life events are stored and remembered in the astral body and can act from there on the physical body.

aura. Our subtle multidimensional energy body that is vibrating the living blueprint for our physical body and life. It is alternately made up of lines of light and a diffused cloud-like light matter comprising the structures and layers that is the human aura and the underpinning of our human body. The aura has its own intelligence, color, memory and is dynamic. It is also referred to in this book as our *bioenergetic computer*, as it can be updated and restored beyond its original intended version. The aura is the "go-between," negotiating our spiritual and physical reality through its chakra system, which is a vital part of the aura.

ascended masters. Former human beings who have reached spiritual enlightenment through initiations and trials. Ascended masters are now in service to humanity for the greater good of all.

avatar. A conscious manifestation of a deity in physical form. Avatars know and have never forgotten that they are God beings in physical presence and are the most humble servants of the light.

chakra system. A vital part of the aura. Chakras are energetic conical structures that are made up of spinning vortices. The chakras govern and support specific aspects of our human being and function physically, emotionally, mentally, and spiritually by regulating the flow of life-force energy or prana in the aura and the body. In the heart flame healing system, I address the seven main chakras, which have a front and back aspect that are separate from each other and that have different function.

A secondary chakra system governs all joints and organs of the body. The shoulders, wrists, knees, and toe joints all have chakras that can be restored to original functioning, which will immediately improve functioning and can relieve pain in the affected joint.

core star. The deepest dimension of our human being. Here we are pure light and delight in our dreams that are pulsing forth from the heart of God. It is the radiance of our God self.

deity. A divine being, an individualized living light aspect of God.

divine discontent. A feeling of uneasiness, emptiness, wanting, or desiring, the focus of which is not quite clear yet. It is usually the feeling before longing becomes conscious.

divine genius of God. The God-given genius intelligence present within and unique to each individual. To bring forth the divine genius of God, one has to claim it, nurture it, and activate it with practice and discipline. One's longing or inner heart's dream always points in the direction to one's personal divine genius of God.

God self. The ultimate creative essence of our being.

God source. That from which all things spring forth, the source of all.

hara. A dynamic, alive energetic line a level deeper than the aura. The hara holds within itself the code for the fulfillment of our life. It runs through the center of our bones and in front of the spine.

harmonizing. A life and healing skill that allows one to come into harmony with others, oneself, a group, or an event. It is done by intention, declaration, and finally by being in harmony.

heart flame. The spiritual fire of your longing, the sacred flame that burns within your heart of hearts, lighting the way for your inner heart's dream to be fulfilled. If invoked and focused upon, the heart flame will burn away impurities and traumas. The heart flame resides within your upper heart chakra and burns for that which cannot be denied. It is intimately connected to the fulfillment of your purpose.

healing presence. A being that can initiate healing upon command or by its presence.

human energy field. The dynamic energy field than not only emanates from the living human body but also helps to sustain it. The field disintegrates at the time of death.

inner heart's dream. The dream that lives within your heart of hearts, the dream to fulfill your life with what truly matters to you.

longing. See also **heart flame**. Longing refers to your sacred longing to fulfill your life—to bring forth that which lives in your heart of hearts. It is your true desire to live the purpose of your life.

merging. An energetic, alchemical occurrence of becoming one with another in feeling, emotion, or physical sensation.

multidimensional support team (MDST). Individual teams assembled from the living light aspect of God that are available to us in all matters of life on earth. Our MDST is available upon request and through prayer to anyone who asks based in positive reality, especially if he or she is serving the greater good of all. Team members may be deities, angels, ascended masters, or teachers who are still embodied on earth.

past life. A life (of the self) that was lived in the distant past.

past-life overlay. The experience of a past-life trauma that one has gotten used to in present life, like a chronic pain or personality trait.

past-life trauma. Unresolved trauma from a past-life experience that is interfering in present life with pain or misconception.

pendulum. A dowsing tool that is used to verify spiritual guidance. A pendulum can also be used to connect to the innate wisdom of the physical body and its needs.

positive reality. The creative and supportive experience of life that is free of anger, blame, and victimhood. It usually supports the greater good of all.

sacred human heart. The divine aspect of our physical human heart—the heartbeat, the pulse of life itself present within each human being—that connects us all.

soul. The soul is at the core of our existence and is eternally connected to source or God.

spiritual reality. The subtle dimensions that are overarching our human reality. These dimensions are alive with divine intelligence, deities, guides, angels, and other beings of the light, which are available by request to guide our human reality in all matters. Spiritual reality or dimension can be accessed through our sacred human heart, in prayer, and in positive reality.

soul seat. Part of the hara and the place in the body where our longing resides. It is located at the sternum in the chest and at the upper heart chakra.

spirit surgeons. Spirit doctors who perform spiritual surgeries that are beyond the scope of a healer or healing presence in the physical dimension. They are highly specialized beings and often have been in physical service to humanity as surgeons or doctors before assisting others from the spiritual dimension.

soul trauma. A traumatic past-life experience that was so deep and sustained that it scarred the soul and left the being with a pervasive feeling of diminishment.

spirit guides. Our invisible companions who have been assigned to us since before birth. They help us fulfill our purpose—the reason we have incarnated this time around.

the void. The empty space of pure creative potential.

universal intelligence. The intelligence of life itself everywhere, also source.

About the Author

Karin Inana is a divine healing presence. Clairvoyant, heart centered and highly empathic, she acts as a bridge linking spiritual and human reality.

After graduating Brennan Healing Science School, she mastered the art of healing by using all facets of the multidimensional field.

Working closely with her multidimensional support team, Karin Inana shares her high-level healing work globally. She currently lives in Calabasas, California.

CPSIA information can be obtained
at www.ICGtesting.com
Printed in the USA
LVHW050433240920
666973LV00001B/84

9 781982 214760